THE ULTIMATE

AIR FRYER COOKBOOK

Low Fat & Delicious Air Fryer Recipes for Busy Families to Cook Homemade Meals |Your Ultimate Guide to Effortless Air Frying |Full Color Book

Joni B. Ryan

Copyright© 2024 By Joni B. Ryan
All Rights Reserved

This book is copyright protected. It is only for personal use.
You cannot amend, distribute, sell, use,
quote or paraphrase any part of the content within this book,
without the consent of the author or publisher.
Under no circumstances will any blame or
legal responsibility be held against the publisher,
or author, for any damages, reparation,
or monetary loss due to the information contained within this book,
either directly or indirectly.

Disclaimer Notice:

Please note the information contained within this
document is for educational and entertainment purposes only.
All effort has been executed to present accurate,
up to date, reliable, complete information.
No warranties of any kind are declared or implied.
Readers acknowledge that the author is not engaged
in the rendering of legal,
financial, medical or professional advice.
The content within this book has been derived from various sources.
Please consult a licensed professional before attempting any
techniques outlined in this book.
By reading this document,
the reader agrees that under no circumstances is the
author responsible for any losses,
direct or indirect,
that are incurred as a result of the use of the
information contained within this document, including,
but not limited to, errors, omissions, or inaccuracies.

TABLE OF
CONTENTS

- **01**   **INTRODUCTION**
- **07**   Chapter 1: BREAKFAST
- **14**   Chapter 2: POULTRY
- **22**   Chapter 3: MEAT
- **30**   Chapter 4: FISH & SEAFOOD
- **38**   Chapter 5: BEANS & GRAINS
- **46**   Chapter 6: VEGAN & VEGETARIAN
- **54**   Chapter 7: LIGHT BITES & SIDE DISHES
- **61**   Chapter 8: DESSERTS
- **66**   Bonus Recipe
- **76**   **INDEX**

INTRODUCTION

I embraced the world of air frying in my kitchen a few years ago. My transitioning from traditional cooking methods to the magic of hot air circulation has not only improved my cooking routine but has also provided healthier and more enjoyable culinary options. From classic comfort foods such as fish & chips to more sophisticated dishes, the air fryer is proving its versatility time and again. Baking casseroles to perfection, grilling vegetables and meats to achieve that ideal sear – the possibilities seem endless!

Forget greasy meat and soggy vegetables – the Air Fryer revolution is here! Chicken skin that crackles, roasted vegs that glisten, and cookies that melt in your mouth, get ready for a memorable Air Fryer experience in the comfort of your home! Air fryers are popular kitchen tools that use hot air to cook food, making them a healthier alternative to deep-frying. It can help promote weight loss and reduce unhealthy fat intake when used according to instructions. Air Fryers produce crispy, golden delights using little to no oil; they can turn ordinary frozen food into restaurant-worthy feasts in a fraction of the time! Embrace the ease of the air fryer, creating that irresistible fluffy-on-the-inside and crispy-on-the-outside, bites!

The first thing that struck me about air frying is reduced dependence on oil. Air Fryers require a fraction of the oil, resulting in a lower calorie content. Air frying uses hot air circulation to cook food, requiring significantly less oil than most cooking methods, especially deep frying. Since it is a fast cooking method, air frying tends to retain more nutrients in food compared to most cooking methods; it is well known that prolonged exposure to high temperatures can lead to nutrient loss. In addition to being a healthier alternative to deep-frying, air frying is also a fast and energy-efficient method, rapidly blasting hot air around your food. Gone are the long waiting times associated with oven baking or stovetop simmering; my air fryer is a champion of modern cooking for me!

Air fryers can be used to prepare a wide variety of foods, from simple breakfast meals to hearty side dishes and even desserts. Thanks to user-friendly control panels, they are easy to operate, making them a convenient addition to any kitchen! Clean-up is a breeze, adding another layer of convenience to my cooking adventure! I love the fact that the post-cooking ritual requires much less effort compared to the usual hassles of traditional cooking! Now, ditch the fat and embrace the flavour – this recipe collection is your game-changer for mastering this cutting-edge technique. From easy, traditional breakfast to light bites and sweet delights, I've got you covered with 100 irresistible dishes! Plus, I'll guide you through everything you need to know, from choosing the right ingredients to mastering cooking temperatures and times. You will learn how to cook lighter versions of your favourite restaurant foods and save calories without losing flavour and aroma. If you are an Air Fryer novice, you will unleash your inner chef with this comprehensive cookbook! Trust me, your attitude to cooking will never be the same again!

My Air Fryer become a staple in my kitchen as a time-saving and health-conscious companion! Imagine crispy and fluffy roasties, sizzling wings, and juicy steaks in minutes. And it's not just for the classics – this cookbook contains modern and innovative recipes, from fluffy flapjack to decadent desserts like brownies and fruity crumbles. Now, grab your apron and let's dive into the magical world of air-frying!

5 Things You Should Know About Using Your Air Fryer

Air fryers offer crispy, delicious food without the unhealthy downsides of deep frying. But what features should you look for when choosing your perfect one? Here are 5 main features of an Air Fryer:

1. Rapid Air Circulation.

This revolutionary technology lies in heating elements and powerful fans. Hot air rapidly circulates the food, creating a Maillard reaction (i.e. the browning). This effect delivers that crisp exterior and moist and tender interior. Keep in mind that many recipes benefit from shaking or flipping the food halfway through the cooking process.

2. Convenience.

Air fryers can easily fit on kitchen countertops, even if you have limited kitchen space. They have non-stick cooking baskets that are easy to clean. Plus, some parts are dishwasher-safe. Most air fryers feature a digital display and user-friendly controls; this makes it easy to set and adjust cooking parameters with precision. In fact, the timers help prevent overcooking and undercooking, allowing users to focus on other tasks while their food cooks. And last but not least, modern air fryers come with safety features such as cool-touch handles and overheat protection. Lovely!

3. Versatility.

Air fryers aren't just for frying; you can bake, roast, reheat, dehydrate, and grill your food. From meat and vegetables to vegan dishes and even desserts, the possibilities are endless! Some air fryers come with accessories like racks or skewers. Familiarize yourself with these accessories because they can expand the range of recipes you can prepare!

Many air fryer models come with pre-programmed settings for popular dishes. These features make it even easier for users to prepare a variety of meals without any fuss!

4. Reduced Oil Usage and Healthy Cooking.

One of the biggest advantages of air fryers is their ability to cook food with minimal to no oil. This means significantly fewer calories and fat compared to traditional cooking methods. This method produces a crispy outer layer while maintaining the moisture inside. To make things easier and prevent sticking, consider using baking parchment paper or tin foil with perforations. This also helps protect and keep the non-stick coating of the air fryer basket in perfect shape.

5. Time Efficiency and Temperature Control.

Air fryers typically cook food faster than conventional ovens. The rapid air circulation and the compact cooking space contribute to quicker cooking times. Most devices come with adjustable temperature settings, allowing you to control the cooking process.

How to Clean an Air Fryer in Five Easy Steps

Cleaning your Air Fryer regularly is essential to maintain its performance and ensure the longevity of your machine. It is essential to perform routine cleaning after each use to prevent the build-up of grease and food particles. Here's a general guide on how to clean an air fryer:

1. Before cleaning, always unplug the air fryer. Then, allow the Air Fryer to cool down for at least 30 minutes before starting the cleaning process.

2. Take the cooking basket out and shake off any food particles. Wash the basket and tray with hot water, mild dish soap, and a non-abrasive sponge. If they have stubborn, stuck-on food, you can soak it in warm, soapy water to help loosen the debris. You can use a mixture of water and a small amount of vinegar or baking soda.

3. Next, wipe down the interior with a damp cloth. Be gentle and avoid using abrasive materials and scouring pads that could damage the coating. If your Air Fryer has a drip tray, empty and clean it as needed.

4. Use a soft brush to clean the heating element. Be careful - it is a sensitive component.

5. Lastly, wipe down the exterior of your Air Fryer with a damp cloth. You can use soapy water if needed.

Are Air Fryers Safe?

In short, Air Fryers can be a valuable addition to every kitchen, but it's important to be aware of potential risks. By using them responsibly and making informed choices, you can enjoy air-fried food while minimizing potential disadvantages.

1. Health Concerns and Acrylamides.

Air frying is a high-heat cooking method, which can form acrylamides that are possibly carcinogenic to humans. While the health risks are still being researched, minimizing acrylamides in food is advisable. It is essential to avoid overcooking, soak starchy foods before cooking, and avoid scratching the non-stick coating. Opt for PFOA-free models and avoid nonstick coatings containing PFAS ("forever chemicals"). Reduce sodium intake and focus on using fresh seasonings and aromatics. As with any cooking method, it's essential to maintain a balanced diet and incorporate a variety of food groups.

Beginners may face challenges in terms of overcooking or unevenly cooked food. It's essential to follow recipes and guidelines to avoid health issues.

2 Safety Risks.

As with any electrical appliance, there is a risk of different electrical malfunctions. Air fryers reach high temperatures, so be careful and use heat-resistant gloves and utensils. Further, air fryers can cause fires, so make sure to follow safety precautions. Air Fryers may emit smoke so ensure proper ventilation in your home.

3. Environmental Impact.

Air fryers are electrical devices so they contribute to your energy footprint. Opt for energy-efficient models! Electrical devices pollute the environment; consider repairing or donating them instead of discarding them prematurely.

Tips and Tricks for Air Fryers

Maximizing the potential of your Air Fryer involves more than just following guidelines and recipes. I have some valuable tips and tricks to help you get the most out of your machine:

1. While one of the best advantages of an air fryer is using less oil, a light coating on your food and cooking basket will enhance that sought-after deliciousness and crispiness. However, keep in mind that using too little oil can result in dry food. Use a cooking spray in a bottle to evenly distribute oil. For delicate items such as pastries, consider brushing a small amount of oil directly on the food; this will help achieve a golden texture without compromising the delicate nature of these items.

2. Preheating the air fryer for a few minutes before cooking can help achieve better and more consistent results.

3. Avoid overcrowding the cooking basket to promote even cooking. Give each item some space so that hot air can circulate around your food, ensuring a crispy texture.

4. Shaking the cooking basket or flipping your food halfway through the cooking time will contribute to even cooking on all sides.

5. Use baking parchment for easy clean-up and better baking results. It is especially important for the items that might stick to the bottom or that can leak through the basket.

6. Every air fryer is different. So, keep a close eye on your food, especially during the first few attempts! Adjust the temperature and cooking time based on your appliance and follow the recipes and general guidelines. Adjusting cooking parameters to suit your preferences will help you achieve the best results. Practice makes perfect! Most air fryers include features like automatic shut-off when the cooking cycle is complete or when the basket is removed.

7. Pat dry meat and vegetables before placing them in the cooking basket. Excess moisture can impact their crispiness! Let the meat or poultry rest for a few minutes after cooking to enhance flavours. This step is essential, especially for dishes like roasts and steaks!

8. Make sure to cook in batches rather than overcrowding the basket. This ensures that each item will cook evenly so you will be able to achieve the best results with your Air Fryer! You will find the right balance by experimenting with the amount of food!

9. Be creative and do not limit yourself to

traditional fried foods. Experiment with baked goods, vegan foods like tempeh and tofu, and even desserts like cakes. Get creative with your favourite seasonings. Try different aromatics or marinades to customize the taste of your meals.

10. Some air fryers come with accessories like skewers or trays. Invest in good quality accessories like spatulas, racks, and bakeware designed for your specific air fryer model. Experiment with bakeware to optimize the cooking of different types of food.

Frequently Asked Questions (Around 10 questions)

1. Why should I use an Air Fryer?

It offers a healthier cooking alternative by reducing the need for excessive oil, resulting in lower fat content. It is also an efficient way to cook a variety of dishes!

2. Is Air Fryer suitable for all types of food?

Absolutely! Air Fryers are extremely versatile, offering a wide range of foods. This cookbook will guide you through various recipes so everyone will be pleased.

3. How do I convert traditional recipes for use in my Air Fryer?

Reduce the cooking temperature by about 15 degrees C compared to traditional oven temperatures. Air fryers cook food faster due to the efficient circulation of hot air. Further, shorten the cooking time – start by reducing the cooking time by 20% and be sure to check for doneness. Reduce the amount of oil used in the recipe; use a cooking spray or lightly brush oil on the food and the bottom of the cooking basket. Air fryers work best when there's less moisture, so reduce the amount of sauce and other liquids in your traditional recipes. And last but not least, cut ingredients into uniform sizes. Internal temperatures may differ from traditional cooking methods, so it's essential to ensure that the food is thoroughly cooked

4 Can I use my Air Fryer for baking, roasting, and dehydrating?

Yes, yes, and yes! Air fryers can function as ovens, making them suitable for baking and roasting. Plus, some models include the "Dehydrate" function. The cookbook will include a diverse range of recipes so be my guest!

5. Can I cook frozen food directly in my Air Fryer?

Absolutely! This fabulous machine can prepare frozen foods to perfection if you follow a few simple rules:

• Preheat the machine. This will help ensure that your food cooks evenly. Most Air Fryers will take about 5 minutes to preheat.

• Increase the cooking time by a few minutes. Frozen food will take slightly longer to cook than fresh or thawed food.

• Don't overcrowd the basket. Arrange your food in a single layer, if possible.

• You may need to add a little bit of oil; it will help to prevent sticking and promote browning.

• Shake the basket halfway through cooking.

• Check the food for doneness a few minutes before the recommended cooking time. Use a food thermometer to check for doneness, especially with meats.

Some examples of frozen foods that cook well in the air fryer include chips, fish fillets, calamari, burgers, chicken nuggets, onion rings, and hashbrowns.

6. Do I need special ingredients for Air Fryer recipes?

While some recipes in this collection may suggest specific ingredients to achieve the best results, most air fryer recipes can be made with commonly available ingredients found in your local stores!

7. Is preheating necessary for an Air Fryer?

Preheating is recommended for some recipes to ensure even cooking, but it is not mandatory at all! In this cookbook, I will specify when preheating is necessary.

8. Is air frying healthier than deep frying?

Air frying uses significantly less oil than deep frying, making it a healthier option. Air Fryers use hot air circulation to cook food, requiring only a minimal amount of oil to achieve a great texture. On the other hand, deep frying involves submerging food in a significant amount of oil, producing higher fat and calorie content.

This makes air-fried dishes a potentially healthier option for those looking to manage their calorie intake. To sum up, it's still essential for you to be mindful of the overall fat content of your meals.

9. Is it safe to cook raw meat in my Air Fryer?

Absolutely! You can safely cook raw meat in Air Fryers, including poultry, beef and fish, as long as you reach the necessary internal temperature for food safety. Always follow recommended cooking times and temperatures as well as use a meat thermometer.

10. Are Air Fryers energy-efficient compared to traditional methods?

Air fryers are generally more energy-efficient than traditional ovens. They cook food faster, reducing overall energy consumption! Consequently, it may contribute to a healthier environment! Win-win!

1
BREAKFAST

Spiced Devilled Eggs

Prep time: 10 minutes / Cook time: 15 minutes / Serves 6 | Per Serving: Calories: 124 | Fat: 9.7g | Carbs: 1.4g | Fibre: 0.3g | Protein: 7.5g

Ingredients
- 6 medium eggs, at room temperature
- 2 tbsp soft white cheese, chilled
- 2 tbsp mayonnaise, chilled
- 1 tsp English mustard
- 1/2 tsp sweet paprika
- Sea salt flakes and ground black pepper, to taste
- A few drops of Tabasco
- 2 tsp coriander leaves, finely chopped

Instructions
1. Place the wire rack in the Air Fryer basket; lower the eggs onto the wire rack.
2. Cook the eggs at 130 degrees C for 15 minutes.
3. Transfer the eggs to an ice-cold water bath to stop cooking. Peel the eggs under cold running water; slice the eggs into halves and separate the egg yolks from the whites.
4. Mash egg yolks with chilled cheese, mayonnaise, English mustard, paprika, salt, black pepper, and Tabasco; spoon the yolk mixture into egg white shells.
5. Arrange devilled eggs on a nice serving tray, garnish them with fresh coriander, and enjoy!

Two Grain Baked Porridge

Prep time: 10 minutes / Cook time: 20 minutes / Serves 4 | Per Serving: Calories: 549 | Fat: 21.7g | Carbs: 78.4g | Fibre: 14g | Protein: 15.5g

Ingredients
- 1 tsp coconut oil
- 150g rye flakes
- 200g porridge oats
- 1 tbsp chia seeds
- 200ml full-fat coconut milk
- 1 large egg, beaten
- 50ml apple sauce
- 50ml agave syrup
- 1/4 tsp ground cinnamon
- A pinch of sea salt

Instructions
1. Brush the inside of a baking tin with coconut oil. Thoroughly combine all the Ingredients and then, spoon the mixture into the prepared baking tin.
2. Bake your porridge at 180 degrees C for 20 minutes.
3. Divide the porridge between four serving bowls; garnish them with fruits and nuts, if desired.

Devour!

Pumpkin English Muffins

Prep time: 10 minutes / Cook time: 20 minutes / Serves 6 | Per Serving: Calories: 369 | Fat: 19.4g | Carbs: 38.1g | Fibre: 3.9g | Protein: 14.8g

Ingredients
- 100g wholemeal flour
- 100g rolled oats, plus extra for sprinkling
- 1 tsp bicarbonate of soda
- 1 tsp pumpkin spice mix
- 80g golden syrup
- 1 large egg, beaten
- 150g pumpkin puree
- 30ml coconut oil
- 60ml natural yoghurt

Instructions
1. Very lightly butter 6 muffin cases.
2. In a bowl, thoroughly combine all the dry ingredients. In a separate bowl, whisk the liquid ingredients.
3. Slowly and gradually, add the liquid mixture to the dry ingredients. Spoon the batter into the prepared muffin cases. Place muffin cases in the cooking basket.
4. Bake your muffins at 170 degrees C for 20 minutes.
5. Let your muffins cool on a rack for about 10 minutes before serving.

Enjoy!

Eggy Bread with a Twist

Prep time: 10 minutes / Cook time: 16 minutes / Serves 2 | Per Serving: Calories: 392 | Fat: 24g | Carbs: 36g | Fibre: 1.9g | Protein: 8.8g

Ingredients
- 1 large egg
- 2 tbsp double cream
- 2 tbsp golden caster sugar
- 1/2 tsp cinnamon powder
- 1/2 tsp ground cloves
- 1 tbsp coconut oil, room temperature
- 2 medium croissants, halved lengthwise

Instructions
1. Line the base of the coking basket with baking parchment.
2. In a mixing bowl, whisk the eggs, cream, sugar, cinnamon, cloves, and coconut oil.
3. Now, dip the croissant halves in the custard mixture until they are well coated on all sides. Lower both croissants into the cooking basket.
4. Bake your croissants at 180 degrees C for 16 minutes, turning them over halfway through the cooking time.

Bon appétit!

British Chelsea Bun

Prep time: 10 minutes / Cook time: 13 minutes / Serves 6 | Per Serving: Calories: 406 | Fat: 21g | Carbs: 50.4g | Fibre: 2.9g | Protein: 5.1g

Ingredients
- 320g ready-rolled puff pastry
- 2 tbsp ground cinnamon
- 100g currants
- 4 tbsp golden caster sugar
- 1 medium egg, beaten
- 100g confectioner's sugar

Instructions
1. Line a baking tray with baking parchment. Unravel the pastry on a lightly floured work surface.
2. Mix the cinnamon, currants and sugar in a bowl.
3. Sprinkle the cinnamon mixture all over the top of your pastry. Brush a little of the beaten egg over the pastry border.
4. Roll the pastry up to create a log; slice it into 6 rolls. Lower the rolls onto the prepared baking trays.
5. Brush them with the remaining beaten egg.
6. Bake your buns at 180 degrees C for 13 minutes, turning them over halfway through the cooking time. Bake in batches if needed.
7. Meanwhile, mix the confectioner's sugar with 2 tablespoons of water. Drizzle your icing over the rolls and enjoy!

Oat Pots with Berries and Almonds

Per Serving: Calories: 470 | Fat: 24.8g | Carbs: 56.6g | Fibre: 7.8g | Protein: 11g

Ingredients
- 150g instant oats
- 2 medium bananas, peeled and mashed
- 1/2 teaspoon ground cinnamon
- 1 tsp pure vanilla extract
- A pinch of grated nutmeg
- A pinch of kosher salt
- 50ml clear honey
- 1 tbsp coconut oil
- 150ml full-fat coconut milk
- 100g mixed berries
- 50g almonds, slivered

Instructions
1. In a mixing bowl, thoroughly combine the oats, bananas, spices, honey, coconut oil, and coconut milk.
2. Spoon the mixture into lightly greased muffin cases.
3. Bake your oats in the preheated Air Fryer at 190 degrees C for about 6 minutes. Top them with berries and almonds; continue to bake for a further 5 to 6 minutes.
4. Serve with a splash of coconut milk, if desired.

Bon appétit!

Prune & Gorgonzola Polenta Stacks

Prep time: 10 minutes / Cook time: 25 minutes / Serves 5   Per Serving: Calories: 334 | Fat: 11.8g | Carbs: 52.2g | Fibre: 1.7g | Protein: 11g

Ingredients
1. 500ml vegetable stock
2. 100g quick-cook polenta
3. 1 tbsp butter, melted
4. 1 tsp rosemary, chopped
5. 1 tbsp thyme, chopped
6. Sea salt and ground black pepper, to taste
7. 9 large prunes, pitted and cut in half lengthways
8. 120g gorgonzola
9. Pomegranate molasses, to drizzle (optional)

Instructions
1. In a saucepan, bring the vegetable stock to a rapid boil. Immediately turn the heat to a gentle simmer; gradually and carefully, stir in the polenta, butter, and spices.
2. Let it simmer, for about 5 minutes, uncovered, whisking continuously to avoid lumps. Pour your polenta into a deep baking tray and let it cool completely.
3. Once the polenta is chilled in your fridge, cut it into 9 squares, using a sharp oiled knife.
4. Arrange polenta squares in the cooking basket. Bake polenta squares in the preheated Air Fryer at 190 degrees C for about 20 minutes.
5. Thread a cocktail stick through each prune and cheese piece; place them on hot polenta squares. Drizzle with a little of the pomegranate molasses, if desired.

Bon appétit!

Crispy Bacon Hash Browns

Prep time: 10 minutes / Cook time: 31 minutes / Serves 5   Per Serving: Calories: 233 | Fat: 16.6g | Carbs: 12.2g | Fibre: 1.9g | Protein: 8.9g

Ingredients
1. 200g waxy potato (such as Charlotte)
2. 4 large eggs, whisked
3. 100g onion, peeled and chopped
4. 100g carrots, trimmed and grated
5. 100g bacon lardons
6. Sea salt and ground black pepper, to taste
7. 30g butter, melted

Instructions
1. Boil the potatoes for 15 minutes; drain. Peel the potatoes and coarsely grate them into a bowl.
2. Add the potatoes, along with the other ingredients, to the mixing bowl. Mix to combine well and divide the mixture between lightly greased muffin cases.
3. Lower the muffin cases into the cooking basket. Bake hash brown cups in the preheated Air Fryer at 180 degrees C for 16 minutes.

Bon appétit!

Breakfast Burrito Bowl

Prep time: 10 minutes / Cook time: 22 minutes / Serves 4 Per Serving: Calories: 445 | Fat: 29.2g | Carbs: 35.1g | Fibre: 8.8g | Protein: 13.8g

Ingredients
1. 2 tsp groundnut oil
2. 4 medium eggs
3. 4 whole-meal tortilla wraps, cut into wedges
4. 2 medium avocado, halved
5. 2 rashers bacon
6. 100g baby spinach
7. Sea salt and red pepper flakes, to taste
8. 2 tsp chipotle paste

Instructions
1. Spray tartlet moulds with 1 teaspoon of groundnut oil. Then, crack an egg in each tartlet mould.
2. Air fry the eggs at 190 degrees C for 6 minutes, until set.
3. After that, toss the tortilla wedges with the remaining 1 teaspoon of groundnut oil, salt, and pepper to taste. Then, air fry your tortillas at 175 degrees C for approximately 3 minutes.
4. Flip the chips and cook for another 3 minutes or until browned and crisp.
5. Cook the bacon at 200 degrees C for 10 minutes
6. Place the avocado halves on a cutting board; now, whack the pit with the sharp end of the knife to remove it easily. Cut your avocado into slices.
7. To assemble your bowls: divide fried eggs, bacon, avocado slices, spinach, and tortilla chips between 4 serving bowls.
8. Drizzle them with chipotle paste and enjoy!

Breakfast Bars with Seeds

Prep time: 10 minutes / Cook time: 16 minutes / Serves 6 Per Serving: Calories: 380 | Fat: 22.7g | Carbs: 40.5g | Fibre: 4.4g | Protein: 8g

Ingredients
- 30g sunflower seed
- 30g pumpkin seeds
- 30g hemp seeds, hulled
- 150g oats
- 60g Sultana
- 80g coconut oil, softened
- 100g honey

Instructions
1. In a mixing bowl, thoroughly combine all Ingredients until everything is well combined.
2. Spoon the mixture into a parchment-lined roasting tin; press down the mixture with a wide spatula.
3. Bake your bars in the preheated Air Fryer at 180 degrees C for 16 minutes.
4. Let it cool before slicing it into bars.

Bon appétit!

Haggis Potato Cakes with Eggs

Prep time: 10 minutes / Cook time: 31 minutes / Serves 4 | Per Serving: Calories: 408 | Fat: 21.7g | Carbs: 33.7g | Fibre: 3.4g | Protein: 18.8g

Ingredients
1. 400g floury potatoes, cut into 3 cm chunks
2. Sea salt and ground black pepper, to taste
3. 200g haggis
4. 1 shallot, chopped
5. 100g panko breadcrumbs
6. 1 tbsp olive oil
7. 4 small eggs

Instructions
1. Boil the potatoes in a pan of salted water for about 11 minutes; mash until smooth. Season with salt and pepper to taste.
2. In the meantime, cook the haggis following pack Instructions. Break them into chunks with a fork; fold through the mash with shallot.
3. Form into four cakes and coat them in the breadcrumbs and olive oil.
4. Air fry potato cakes in the preheated Air Fryer at 180 degrees C for 6 minutes.
5. Place the wire rack in the Air Fryer basket; lower the eggs onto the wire rack. Cook the eggs at 130 degrees C for 14 minutes.
6. Serve the cakes topped with eggs and enjoy!

Breakfast Masala Frittata

Prep time: 10 minutes / Cook time: 14 minutes / Serves 4 | Per Serving: Calories: 214 | Fat: 17.7g | Carbs: 4.5g | Fibre: 1.7g | Protein: 10.6g

Ingredients
- 6 large eggs, beaten
- 4 tbsp double cream
- 2 tbsp olive oil
- 3 spring onions, sliced
- 1 tbsp Madras curry paste
- 1 large tomato, diced
- 1 red chilli, deseeded and finely chopped

Instructions
1. In a bowl, whisk the eggs until frothy; fold in the double cream and mix to combine. Fold in the other Ingredients and whisk until everything is well incorporated.
2. Spoon the frittata mixture into a lightly oiled baking tray.
3. Bake your frittata in the preheated Air Fryer at 180 degrees C for 14 minutes.
4. Cut warm frittata into 4 wedges and serve immediately.

Bon appétit!

2
POULTRY

Honey Hot Wings

Prep time: 10 minutes + marinating time / Cook time: 28 minutes / Serves 4 — Per Serving: Calories: 334 | Fat: 6.7g | Carbs: 14.5g | Fibre: 0.4g

Ingredients
- 8 chicken wings, skin-on
- 1 tsp smoked paprika
- 1 tsp garlic granules
- 1 tbsp cornflour
- Glaze:
- 3 tbsp honey
- 4 tbsp sriracha
- 1 tbsp cider vinegar

Directions
1. Pat dry chicken wings with tea towels.
2. Tip the chicken wings into a large bowl and scatter over spices; toss to coat on all sides and keep the wings chilled overnight.
3. Arrange the wings in the cooking basket in a single layer, fleshy-side down. Scatter over cornflour.
4. Air fry them at 380 degrees F for 22 minutes until the skin is blistered and crisp.
5. In the meantime, whisk the glaze Ingredients until uniform and smooth.
6. Remove the wings from the Air Fryer and brush them with the glaze. Air fry for another 6 minutes until the glaze is starting to char a little.

Bon appétit!

Tandoori-ish Chicken Thighs

Prep time: 10 minutes / Cook time: 40 minutes / Serves 6 — Per Serving: Calories: 486 | Fat: 32.7g | Carbs: 5.5g | Fibre: 0.4g | Protein: 41g

Ingredients
- 6 medium chicken thighs, skin-on, bone-in
- 1 tbsp tomato purée
- 500ml full-fat natural yoghurt
- 2 large garlic cloves, grated
- 2 tsp ground cumin
- 2 tsp ground coriander
- 2 tsp ground turmeric
- 1 tsp hot chilli powder
- 1 medium lemon, juiced

Instructions
1. In a ceramic bowl, place the chicken thighs with the other ingredients. Cover the bowl and let chicken thighs marinate in your fridge for at least 2 hours. Discard the marinade.
2. Spray the marinated chicken with cooking oil and then, arrange them in the Air Fryer cooking basket.
3. Air fry the chicken thighs at 180 degrees for 40 minutes, flipping them halfway through the cooking time to ensure even browning.

Bon appétit!

Cajun Chicken Traybake

Prep time: 10 minutes / Cook time: 35 minutes / Serves 4   Per Serving: Calories: 766 | Fat: 46.7g | Carbs: 39.5g | Fibre: 4g | Protein: 45.1g

Ingredients

1. 4 chicken legs, skin on and bone in
2. 2 tbsp of olive oil
3. 1 tbsp cajun spice mix
4. Sea salt and ground black pepper, to taste
5. 4 small potatoes, cut into wedges
6. 3 cloves garlic, peeled and smashed
7. 1 tbsp honey
8. 2 tbsp whole-grain mustard

Instructions

1. Preheat your Air Fryer to 200 degrees C.
2. Pat the chicken legs dry with tea towels and rub with 1 tbsp of olive oil.
3. Add spices and place the legs in a single layer in the cooking basket. Cook the chicken legs for 15 minutes, flipping halfway through.
4. Meanwhile, toss the potatoes with the spices, garlic, honey, mustard, and the remaining 1 tbsp of olive oil.
5. After the chicken legs have cooked for 15 minutes, add the potatoes to the cooking basket, arranging them around the chicken. Cook for another 20 minutes and serve warm.

Bon appétit!

Chicken and Halloumi Burgers

Prep time: 10 minutes / Cook time: 32 minutes / Serves 4   Per Serving: Calories: 646 | Fat: 33.7g | Carbs: 43.5g | Fibre: 2.1g | Protein: 42.3g

Ingredients

1. 600g chicken tenders, chopped
2. 1 medium onion, chopped
3. 2 fat garlic cloves, minced
4. 2 tbsp piri-piri sauce
5. 50g panko breadcrumbs
6. Sea salt and ground black pepper, to taste
7. 1/2 tsp paprika
8. 4 burger buns
9. 160g halloumi, sliced into 4 pieces
10. 8 Romaine lettuce
11. 4 tbsp tzatziki

Instructions

1. Thoroughly combine the chicken, onion, garlic, piri-piri sauce, breadcrumbs, and spices. Shape the mixture into four patties and spray them with cooking oil.
2. Add burger patties to the cooking basket. Air fry them at 190 degrees C for about 20 minutes.
3. Warm the buns in the air fryer for about 2 minutes until they are warm.
4. Add the halloumi to the cooking basket and cook for 10 minutes; turn the cheese over halfway through and cook until it's golden.
5. Serve your burgers in the buns topped with halloumi, lettuce, and tzatziki.

Bon appétit!

Roast Turkey Breast

Prep time: 10 minutes / Cook time: 40 minutes / Serves 4 | Per Serving: Calories: 394 | Fat: 7.7g | Carbs: 0.7g | Fibre: 0.2g | Protein: 74.3g

Ingredients
- 1 large single turkey breast (about 1kg in total)
- Sea salt and freshly ground black pepper, to taste
- 1 tsp chilli flakes, crushed
- 2 tsp olive oil
- 2 fat cloves garlic, crushed
- 1 tsp dried oregano
- 1 tsp dried rosemary

Instructions
1. Dry the turkey breast with kitchen paper. Massage the turkey breast with the olive oil and spices.
2. Roast the turkey breast in the preheated Air Fryer at 190 degrees C for 20 minutes.
3. Flip them over and continue cooking for another 20 minutes.
4. Enjoy your meal!

Orange-Glazed Duck Breast

Prep time: 10 minutes / Cook time: 32 minutes / Serves 4 | Per Serving: Calories: 264 | Fat: 10.2g | Carbs: 14.7g | Fibre: 2.8g | Protein: 28.3g

Ingredients
- 600g duck breast
- 1 tsp sunflower oil
- 1/2 tsp cayenne pepper
- Sea salt and ground black pepper, to taste
- Orange Glaze:
- 1 small orange, juiced (clementine or satsuma)
- 30g honey
- 50ml ruby port wine

Instructions
1. Dry the duck breast with kitchen paper. Liberally rub the oil and spices all over the duck breast.
2. Cover the duck breast loosely with foil and lower it into a roasting tray. Roast the duck breast in the preheated Air Fryer at 190 degrees C for 15 minutes.
3. In the meantime, mix the glaze ingredients.
4. Flip the duck breast over, remove the foil, and add the glaze mixture; give a good baste with the glaze. Now, continue cooking for a further 17 minutes.

Enjoy!

Turkey Chorizo Ragù

Prep time: 10 minutes / Cook time: 32 minutes / Serves 4   Per Serving: Calories: 344 | Fat: 20.9g | Carbs: 5.1g | Fibre: 0.8g | Protein: 33.3g

Ingredients
- 1 tbsp olive oil
- 500g turkey breast, chopped
- 120g cooking chorizo, chopped
- 1 large onion, chopped
- 1 large celery rib, chopped
- 2 fat cloves garlic, finely diced
- 1 tbsp Marmite
- 1 tbsp piri-piri sauce
- 1 tsp Italian seasoning mix

Instructions
1. Melt the butter in a nonstick frying pan over medium-high heat. Once hot, cook the turkey and chorizo for about 5 minutes, until no longer pink.
2. Add the remaining vegetables and continue to sauté for 5 minutes more, until just tender.
3. Spoon the veg/ turkey mixture into the lightly-greased baking tray; stir in the remaining ingredients; stir to combine well.
4. Now, lower the baking tray into the Air Fryer cooking basket. Cook your ragù at 180 degrees C for 20 minutes.

Bon appétit!

Baked Chicken Nuggets

Prep time: 10 minutes / Cook time: 25 minutes / Serves 4   Per Serving: Calories: 530 | Fat: 30.1g | Carbs: 24.6g | Fibre: 3.2g | Protein: 38g

Ingredients
- 600g chicken thighs, cut the chicken thighs into nugget-sized pieces
- 160ml natural yoghurt
- 120g mayonnaise
- 2 tbsp tikka masala curry paste 
- 50g crispy onions
- 100g breadcrumbs
- Sea salt and ground black pepper, to taste
- 1 tsp red pepper flakes, crushed
- 1 tsp dried oregano
- 2 tbsp mango chutney

Instructions
1. Add the chicken, yoghurt, curry paste, and mayonnaise to a ceramic bowl. Cover and leave in the fridge to marinate for about 2 hours.
2. In a baking dish, thoroughly combine the dried onions, breadcrumbs, and spices.
3. Turn the marinated chicken pieces in the breadcrumb mix; spray each nugget with the cooking oil.
4. Cook chicken nuggets in the preheated Air Fryer at 390 degrees F for 25 minutes.
5. Serve chicken nuggets with mango chutney.

Bon appétit!

Baked Chicken Fajitas

Prep time: 10 minutes / Cook time: 21 minutes / Serves 4 | Per Serving: Calories: 490 | Fat: 23.1g | Carbs: 29.3g | Fibre: 2.2g | Protein: 27.8g

Ingredients
- 2 chicken fillets (250g each), finely sliced
- 1 large onion, peeled and sliced
- 1 large bell pepper, deseeded and sliced
- 2 tbsp groundnut oil
- 1 tsp smoked paprika
- 1/2 tsp garlic granules
- 1 tsp ground coriander
- 1/2 tsp ground cumin
- A few drizzles of Tabasco sauce
- Sea salt and freshly ground black pepper, to taste
- 4 medium tortillas

Instructions
1. Toss the chicken slices and vegetables with the spices, groundnut oil, and Tabasco.
2. Add the chicken slices to the cooking basket. Air Fry them at 190 degrees C for about 10 minutes.
3. Add the vegetables to the basket and continue to cook for a further 9 minutes. Reserve.
4. Then, warm the tortillas at 170 degrees C for about 2 minutes.
5. Add the chicken and vegetables to the warmed tortillas.

Enjoy your meal!

Chicken Bacon Polpettes

Prep time: 10 minutes / Cook time: 12 minutes / Serves 4 | Per Serving: Calories: 344 | Fat: 13.1g | Carbs: 8.2g | Fibre: 1.2g | Protein: 46.6g

Ingredients
- 600g chicken breasts, chopped
- 2 bacon rashers, chopped
- 1 large bread slice, crustless and chopped
- 1 medium onion, chopped
- 2 garlic cloves, minced
- 1 egg, whisked
- 2 tbsp double cream
- 2 tbsp fresh parsley leaves, chopped
- 2 tbsp fresh cilantro leaves, chopped
- 1 tbsp soy sauce
- Sea salt and ground black pepper, to taste

Instructions
1. Thoroughly combine all of the above Ingredients until everything is well incorporated. Shape the mixture into equal meatballs.
2. Spray a cooking basket with cooking spray.
3. Air fry your meatballs at 360 degrees F for 10 to 12 minutes, shaking the basket periodically to ensure even cooking.

Bon appétit!

Chicken Satay Strips

Prep time: 10 minutes / Cook time: 12 minutes / Serves 4   Per Serving: Calories: 304 | Fat: 16.1g | Carbs: 4.2g | Fibre: 1.1g | Protein: 32.2g

Ingredients
- 600g chicken breast fillets, cut into thick strips
- 1/2 garlic granules
- 1 tsp smoked paprika
- 1 tsp dried oregano
- 1/2 tsp dried basil
- Sea salt and ground black pepper, to taste
- 1 tsp olive oil
- 2 tbsp peanut butter
- 1 tbsp lemon juice
- 1 tsp Madras curry powder
- A few shakes soy sauce

Instructions
1. Toss the chicken strips with the spices and olive oil. (You can tread chicken pieces onto skewers).
2. Add the chicken strips to the cooking basket. Air Fry them at 190 degrees C for about 10 minutes.
3. In the meantime, whisk the remaining ingredients.
4. Baste the chicken with the peanut butter mixture and continue to cook for a further 10 minutes.

Bon appétit!

Cranberry-Glazed Roast Turkey

Prep time: 10 minutes / Cook time: 42 minutes / Serves 4   Per Serving: Calories: 434 | Fat: 17.7g | Carbs: 13.7g | Fibre: 1.2g | Protein: 49.3g

Ingredients
- 900g turkey breast
- Sea salt and freshly ground black pepper, to taste
- 1 tbsp butter
- 1 tsp dried thyme
- Cranberry Glaze:
- 6 tbsp of cranberry jelly
- 30g soft brown sugar
- 50ml port
- 100g of cranberries, fresh or frozen

Instructions
1. Dry the turkey breast with kitchen paper. Liberally rub the spices and butter all over the turkey breast.
2. Cover the turkey breast loosely with foil and lower it into a roasting tray. Roast the turkey breast in the preheated Air Fryer at 190 degrees C for 22 minutes.
3. In the meantime, mix the glaze ingredients.
4. Flip the turkey breast over, remove the foil, and add the glaze mixture. Now, continue cooking for another 20 minutes.

Enjoy!

Herb Chicken Mini Fillets

Per Serving: Calories: 344 | Fat: 16.4g | Carbs: 0.4g | Fibre: 0.2g | Protein: 45.3g

Ingredients
- 900g chicken mini fillets (or tenders)
- 2 tbsp olive oil
- 1 tsp dried thyme
- 1 tsp dried parsley flakes
- 1 tbsp dried rosemary
- 1 fat garlic clove, minced
- Sea salt and ground black pepper, to taste

Instructions
1. Toss chicken mini fillets with olive oil, garlic, and spices.
2. Place the chicken tenders in the cooking basket.
3. Air fry chicken mini fillets at 200 degrees C for about 12 minutes.

Bon appétit!

English Mustard Roast Chicken

Prep time: 10 minutes / Cook time: 40 minutes / Serves 4   Per Serving: Calories: 394 | Fat: 7.7g | Carbs: 0.7g | Fibre: 0.2g | Protein: 74.3g

Ingredients
- 1 large single chicken breast (about 1kg in total)
- 1 tbsp English mustard
- Sea salt and freshly ground black pepper, to taste
- 1 tsp chilli flakes, crushed
- 1 tsp garlic granules
- 1 tsp dried onion flakes
- 1 tsp dried parsley flakes
- 1 tbsp olive oil

Instructions
1. Dry the chicken breast with kitchen paper. Massage the chicken breast with the mustard, olive oil and spices.
2. Roast the chicken breast in the preheated Air Fryer at 190 degrees C for 10 minutes.
3. Flip them over and continue cooking for another 10 minutes.

Bon appétit!

3
MEAT

Parmesan Pork Chops

Per Serving: Calories: 365 | Fat: 14g | Carbs: 3.2g | Fibre: 0.4g | Protein: 53.3g

Ingredients
- 900g pork loin chops, boneless
- 2 tsp olive oil
- 50g Parmesan cheese, grated
- 1 tsp hot paprika
- 1 tsp English mustard powder
- Sea salt and ground black pepper, to taste

Instructions
1. Toss pork loin chops with the other ingredients.
2. Spray the bottom of the Air Fryer cooking basket with cooking oil. Cook pork loin chops at 200 degrees C for 7 minutes.
3. Flip the chops and cook them for a further 7 minutes on the other side.
4. Serve warm and enjoy!

British Pork Sandwich

Prep time: 10 minutes / Cook time: 1 hour / Serves 4

Per Serving: Calories: 464 | Fat: 21.7g | Carbs: 28.2g | Fibre: 2.2g | Protein: 35.3g

Ingredients
- 500g pork loin
- 2 tsp soft butter
- 1 tsp cayenne pepper
- Sea salt and ground black pepper, to taste
- 1 medium apple, cored and sliced
- 100g brie, sliced
- 1 roll brioche

Instructions
1. Toss the pork with the butter and spices.
2. Transfer the pork loin to the Air Fryer cooking basket.
3. Cook the pork loin in your Air Fryer at 200 degrees C for 55 minutes, turning twice to ensure even cooking.
4. After 45 minutes, add apple slices and continue cooking for 10 minutes more. Slice the pork.
5. After that, slice the buns, add the brie, and pop this into the Air Fryer; let it melt away.
6. Layer the rolls with the pork and apple slices. Serve warm and enjoy!

Warm Steak Salad

Prep time: 10 minutes / Cook time: 15 minutes / Serves 4 — Per Serving: Calories: 236 | Fat: 10.7g | Carbs: 8.2g | Fibre: 1.5g | Protein: 27.3g

Ingredients
- 2 (250g) rump steaks
- 2 tsp groundnut oil
- Kosher salt and ground black pepper, to taste
- 1 large tomato, diced
- A large handful of baby spinach
- 100g radishes, sliced
- 100g bean sprouts
- Dressing:
- 1 garlic clove, crushed
- 1 tbsp soft brown sugar
- 1 tbsp fish sauce
- 1/2 lemon, zested and juiced
- 1 tbsp Dijon mustard
- 1 tablespoon soy sauce
- 1 teaspoon hot paprika

Instructions
1. Pat the steak dry using tea towels. Rub the steak with the groundnut oil and season on both sides with salt and pepper.
2. Cook the steak in the preheated Air Fryer at 200 degrees C for 7 minutes; turn on the other side and cook for 7 to 8 minutes more.
3. Meanwhile, whisk all the dressing Ingredients until the brown sugar has dissolved.
4. To assemble the salad, pile the tomato, spinach, and radsihes onto plates; mix with the beansprouts and coriander. Top with the steak and dressing.

Bon appétit!

Old-Fashioned Meatballs

Prep time: 10 minutes / Cook time: 15 minutes / Serves 4 — Per Serving: Calories: 406 | Fat: 25.5g | Carbs: 13.6g | Fibre: 2.6g | Protein: 30.3g

Ingredients
- 300g pork mince (84% lean, 16% fat)
- 300g beef mince (85% lean, 15% fat)
- 50g porridge oats
- 1 tsp rapeseed oil
- 1 medium onion, chopped
- 2 fat garlic cloves, minced
- 1 tbsp English mustard
- 1 tsp sweet paprika
- 1 tsp dried thyme
- 1 tsp ground coriander seeds
- Sea salt and ground black pepper, to taste

Instructions
1. Tip the mince into a mixing bowl, followed by the other ingredients; lightly knead the Ingredients together until everything is well incorporated.
2. Shape the mixture into 8 equal balls (ping-pong-sized).
3. Air fry pork meatballs at 200 degrees C for 15 minutes. Turn the meatballs halfway through the cooking time.

Bon appétit!

Roast Pork Belly

Prep time: 10 minutes / Cook time: 55 minutes / Serves 5 | Per Serving: Calories: 526 | Fat: 53.1g | Carbs: 1.6g | Fibre: 0.7g | Protein: 9.7g

Ingredients
1. 500g pork belly, bone-in, skin scored
2. 1 tbsp hot paprika
3. Sea salt and ground black pepper, to taste
4. 1 star anise
5. 1 tsp cumin seeds

Instructions
1. Ground the spices to a powder using a pestle and mortar. Rub all over the pork belly.
2. Place the pork belly, rind side up, in the cooking basket.
3. Cook the pork belly in the preheated Air Fryer at 200 degrees c for 25 minutes; turn it over and cook at 160 degrees C for another 30 minutes.
4. Let the pork rest on a wire rack for approximately 10 minutes before carving. Then, carve the pork into squares using a sharp, bread knife.

Bon appétit!

Sizzling Spare Ribs

Prep time: 10 minutes / Cook time: 30 minutes / Serves 4 | Per Serving: Calories: 286 | Fat: 13.9g | Carbs: 7.5g | Fibre: 0.4g | Protein: 25.7g

Ingredients
1. 1 (500g) pack pork spare ribs
2. 3 tbsp rum
3. 1 Scotch bonnet chilli, seeded and finely chopped
4. 2 fat garlic cloves, chopped
5. 3 tbsp demerara sugar
6. 3 tbsp tamari sauce
7. 2 tsp English mustard

Instructions
1. Tip the ribs into a ceramic dish. Add the other Ingredients to the dish.
2. Turn the ribs a few times until they're well coated in the marinade ingredients. Let the ribs marinate for at least 1 hour.
3. Add the ribs to a roasting tray. Roast the ribs at 200 degrees C for 20 minutes.
4. Reduce the heat to 190 degrees C, baste the ribs with the reserved marinade, and cook them for a further 10 minutes.

Bon appétit!

BBQ Point end Brisket

Prep time: 10 minutes / Cook time: 30 minutes / Serves 4   Per Serving: Calories: 536 | Fat: 42.1g | Carbs: 1.6g | Fibre: 0.5g | Protein: 35.5g

Ingredients
1. 800g point end brisket
2. 2 tbsp beef rub
3. 100ml BBQ sauce

Instructions
1. Toss the beef with the remaining ingredients; place the beef in the Air Fryer cooking basket.
2. Cook the beef at 200 degrees C for 15 minutes, turn the beef over and continue to cook for a further 15 minutes.

Bon appétit!

Classic Carnitas

Prep time: 10 minutes / Cook time: 1 hour / Serves 4   Per Serving: Calories: 398 | Fat: 17.1g | Carbs: 17.6g | Fibre: 1.5g | Protein: 40.5g

Ingredients
- 600g pork shoulder
- 2 tsp grapeseed oil
- 1 tsp red pepper flakes, crushed
- 2 tsp dried oregano
- 2 tsp ground cumin
- Sea salt and ground black pepper, to taste
- Avocado
- 100g blue cheese, sliced
- 4 medium flour tortillas

Instructions
1. Toss the pork with the oil and spices.
2. Transfer the pork to the Air Fryer cooking basket.
3. Cook the pork loin in your Air Fryer at 200 degrees C for 55 minutes, turning twice to ensure even cooking.
4. Shred the pork with two forks. Layer tortillas with the pork and cheese. Air fry tortillas at 180 degrees C for about 5 minutes until they are crispy and charred and the cheese melts.
5. Serve warm and enjoy!

Nacho Cheeseburgers

Prep time: 10 minutes / Cook time: 25 minutes / Serves 4 Per Serving: Calories: 596 | Fat: 35.7g | Carbs: 25.7g | Fibre: 2.1g | Protein: 42.5g

Ingredients
- 600g beef mince
- 50g bacon lardons
- 1 fat garlic clove, minced
- 1 small onion, chopped
- 2 tbsp BBQ sauce
- Sea salt and ground black pepper, to taste
- 4 (30g) slices cheddar cheese
- 4 tbsp guacamole
- 4 tbsp chipotle mayo
- A small handful salted nachos
- A small bunch of coriander, leaves torn
- 4 sesame seed burger buns

Instructions
1. Mix the beef, bacon, garlic, onion, BBQ sauce, salt, and black pepper until everything is well combined. Form the mixture into four patties.
2. Cook the burgers at 380 degrees F for about 15 minutes or until cooked through.
3. After 10 minutes, turn the burgers over and top each burger with a slice of cheese. Continue to cook until the burgers are cooked through.
4. Serve your burgers on the prepared buns and add the other topping ingredients. Enjoy!

Spicy Mini Meatloaves

Prep time: 10 minutes / Cook time: 25 minutes / Serves 4 Per Serving: Calories: 409 | Fat: 22.7g | Carbs: 24.1g | Fibre: 3.1g | Protein: 27.5g

Ingredients
- 250g lean beef
- 250g pork mince
- 2 thyme leaves, chopped
- 2 fat garlic cloves, crushed
- 1 medium egg, beaten
- 1 carrot, grated
- 1 onion, finely chopped
- 1 small chilli pepper, chopped
- 50g fresh breadcrumbs
- 1 tsp cayenne pepper
- Sea salt and ground black pepper, to taste
- Glaze:
- 150ml passata
- 1 tbsp brown sugar
- 2 tsp Worcestershire sauce

Instructions
1. Mix the meat, thyme, garlic, egg, carrot, onion, chilli, breadcrumbs, and spices.
2. Mix the remaining Ingredients for the glaze.
3. Brush 4 ramekins with cooking oil. Press the meat mixture into them.
4. Cook the beef meatloaves at 380 degrees F for 20 minutes.
5. After that, spread the glaze on the top of each meatloaf; continue to cook for another 5 minutes. Serve with potato mash, if desired.

Bon appétit!

Rump Steak with Gorgonzola

Prep time: 10 minutes / Cook time: 15 minutes / Serves 2   Per Serving: Calories: 630 | Fat: 40.1g | Carbs: 4.1g | Fibre: 0.4g | Protein: 64.5g

Ingredients
- 2 x 250g rump steak, 2-3cm thick
- 1 tbsp grapeseed oil
- 2 fat garlic cloves, crushed
- 1 sprig thyme, chopped
- 1 sprig rosemary, chopped
- Coarse sea salt and ground black pepper, to taste
- 100g gorgonzola cheese, crumbled.

Instructions
1. Pat the steak dry using tea towels. Rub the steak with the other ingredients, except gorgonzola, on both sides.
2. Cook the steak in the preheated Air Fryer at 200 degrees C for 10 minutes; turn on the other side, top with gorgonzola, and cook for a further 5 minutes.

Bon appétit!

Paprika Pork Medallions

4   Per Serving: Calories: 238 | Fat: 5.5g | Carbs: 1.7g | Fibre: 0.6g | Protein: 42.3g

Ingredients
- 800g pork medallions
- 2 tsp unsalted butter
- 1 tsp hot paprika
- 1 tsp sweet paprika
- Sea salt and ground black pepper, to taste

Instructions
1. Toss pork medallions with the other ingredients.
2. Spray the bottom of the Air Fryer cooking basket with cooking oil. Cook pork medallions at 200 degrees C for 7 minutes.
3. Flip the medallions and cook them for a further 7 minutes on the other side.
4. Serve warm and enjoy!

Corned Beef Hash

Prep time: 10 minutes / Cook time: 31 minutes / Serves 4   Per Serving: Calories: 277 | Fat: 13.5g | Carbs: 22.5g | Fibre: 3.9g | Protein: 16g

Ingredients
- 300g Charlotte potatoes
- 100g onion, peeled and chopped
- 100g carrots, trimmed and grated
- 340g can of corned beef, cut into cubes
- 2 tbsp Worcestershire sauce
- 30g butter, melted

Instructions
1. Boil the potatoes for 15 minutes; drain. Peel the potatoes and coarsely grate them into a bowl.
2. Add the potatoes, along with the other ingredients, to the mixing dish. Mix to combine well and press the mixture into a lightly greased baking tray.
3. Lower the baking tray into the cooking basket. Bake corned beef hash in the preheated Air Fryer at 180 degrees C for 16 minutes.
4. At the half point, stir the Ingredients to crisp up. Gently break up the meat and potatoes but not too much. Bon appétit!

Savoury Mince Muffins

Prep time: 10 minutes / Cook time: 25 minutes / Serves 6   Per Serving: Calories: 284 | Fat: 18.1g | Carbs: 12.7g | Fibre: 1.1g | Protein: 17.5g

Ingredients
- 300g pork mince
- 200g lean beef
- 50g crushed crackers
- 1 onion, finely chopped
- 2 garlic cloves, crushed
- 1 medium egg, beaten
- 1 tsp red pepper flakes, crushed
- Sea salt and ground black pepper, to taste
- Glaze:
- 150ml tomato paste
- 2 tsp soy sauce
- 1 tbsp honey

Instructions
1. Mix the meat, crackers, onion, garlic, egg, and spices. Whisk the remaining Ingredients for the glaze.
2. Brush 6 muffin cases with cooking oil. Press the meat mixture into them.
3. Cook your muffins at 380 degrees F for 20 minutes.
4. After that, spread the glaze on the top of each muffin; continue to cook for another 5 minutes. Bon appétit!

4
FISH & SEAFOOD

Fried Breaded Squid Rings (Calamari)

Prep time: 10 minutes / Cook time: 10 minutes / Serves 4 | Per Serving: Calories: 199 | Fat: 5.8g | Carbs: 18.7g | Fibre: 1.1g | Protein: 17.5g

Ingredients
- 300g squid tubes, sliced into rings
- Coarse sea salt and ground black pepper, to taste
- 1 tbsp butter, melted
- 2 tbsp sherry wine
- 2 tbsp fresh lemon juice
- 1 large egg, whisked
- 50g plain flour
- 30g panko breadcrumbs
- 2 garlic cloves, smashed
- 1 tsp paprika
- 1 tsp dried oregano

Instructions
1. Toss the squid with salt, pepper, butter, sherry wine, and lemon juice.
2. Dip them into the flour, followed by the egg and finally into the bread crumb mixture.
3. Air fry your calamari at 200 degrees C for 10 minutes; flip them halfway through the cooking time to ensure even cooking.

Bon appétit!

Roast Fillet of Sea Bass

Prep time: 10 minutes / Cook time: 12 minutes / Serves 4 | Per Serving: Calories: 198 | Fat: 2.8g | Carbs: 20.7g | Fibre: 1g | Protein: 21.5g

Ingredients
- 400g sea bass fillet
- 2 tsp fresh lemon juice
- 2 fat garlic cloves, smashed
- 100g plain flour
- 1 tsp red pepper flakes, crushed
- Coarse sea salt and ground black pepper, to taste

Instructions
1. Toss the fish fillets with lemon juice, garlic, plain flour, red pepper flakes, salt, and black pepper.
2. Lower them into a lightly oiled Air Fryer cooking basket.
3. Cook the fish fillets at 200 degrees C for 12 minutes.

Bon appétit!

Easy Fried Prawns

Prep time: 10 minutes / Cook time: 12 minutes / Serves 4   Per Se

Ingredients
- 500g large prawns, peeled and deveined
- 284ml tub buttermilk
- 200g polenta
- Sea salt and ground black pepper, to taste
- 1 tsp dried parsley flakes
- 1 tsp mustard powder
- 1 tbsp olive oil

Instructions
1. Decant the buttermilk into a bowl and give it a good stir. In another bowl, mix the polenta, salt, pepper, parsley, and mustard powder.
2. Dip each prawn in the buttermilk then coat in the polenta mixture.
3. Arrange the prawns in the Air Fryer basket. Drizzle the olive oil over the prawns.
4. Cook the prawns at 200 degrees C for about 12 minutes, shaking the basket halfway through the cooking time.

Enjoy!

Warm Spicy Salmon Salad

Prep time: 10 minutes / Cook time: 12 minutes / Serves 4   Per Serving: Calories: 244 | Fat: 16.8g | Carbs: 8.3g | Fibre: 2.7g | Protein: 16.5g

Ingredients
- 300g salmon fillets
- Sea salt and ground black pepper, to taste
- 2 tbsp olive oil
- 2 garlic cloves, minced
- 1 bell pepper, sliced
- 2 tbsp cup Kalamata olives, pitted and sliced
- 1/2 lime, juiced
- 1 tsp chilli pepper, minced
- A few handfuls of fresh greens (optional)

Instructions
1. Toss the salmon fillets with salt and black pepper; place them in a lightly oiled cooking basket.
2. Spray the fish with cooking oil.
3. Cook the salmon fillets at 200 degrees C for about 6 minutes. Turn them over and spray the fish with cooking oil on the other side.
4. Continue to cook for a further 6 minutes, until the salmon is just cooked in the middle.
5. Chop the salmon fillets using two forks and add them to a salad bowl; add in the remaining Ingredients and toss to combine.

Bon appétit!

Classic Roast Fish

Per Serving: Calories: 220 | Fat: 9.6g | Carbs: 1.7g | Fibre: 0.3g | Protein: 29.5g

Ingredients
- 500g tuna steaks
- Sea salt and ground black pepper, to taste
- 1 tbsp olive oil
- 2 garlic cloves, crushed
- 1 tsp dried rosemary
- 1 tsp dried thyme
- 1 tsp dried parsley flakes

Instructions
1. Toss the tuna steaks with the other ingredients; place them in a lightly greased cooking basket.
2. Cook tuna steaks at 200 degrees C for about 6 minutes. Turn them over and continue to cook for a further 5 minutes, until the tuna steaks are just cooked in the middle.
3. Serve with fresh herbs scattered over. Bon appétit!

Sticky Garlic Trout

Prep time: 10 minutes / Cook time: 12 minutes / Serves 4   Per Serving: Calories: 255 | Fat: 11.6g | Carbs: 10.4g | Fibre: 0.3g | Protein: 26.3g

Ingredients
- 500g trout, cut into fillets
- 1 tbsp sesame oil
- 1/2 tsp cayenne pepper
- Sea salt and ground black pepper, to taste
- 2 tbsp clear honey
- 2 tsp apple cider vinegar
- 2 fat cloves garlic, smashed

Instructions
1. Toss trout fillets with sesame oil and spices; place them in a lightly greased cooking basket.
2. Whisk the remaining Ingredients in a bowl.
3. Cook your fish at 200 degrees C for 7 minutes.
4. Add the glaze Ingredients and continue to cook for a further 5 minutes, or until the fish flakes when gently pressed.

Bon appétit!

Easy Marinated Swordfish

Prep time: 5 minutes + marinating time / Cook time: 12 minutes / Serves 4 | Per Serving: Calories: 285 | Fat: 16.6g | Carbs: 0.6g | Fibre: 0.1g |

Ingredients
- 600g swordfish steaks
- 50ml dry red wine
- 2 tbsp olive oil
- 2 tsp tamari sauce
- 2 sprigs rosemary
- 1 sprig thyme
- Salt and freshly ground pepper, to taste
- 1 tsp grated lemon peel

Instructions
1. Toss the swordfish steaks with the remaining Ingredients in a ceramic (or glass) dish; cover and let it marinate in your fridge for about 2 hours.
2. Then, reserve the marinade and place the fish in a lightly greased cooking basket.
3. Cook the swordfish steaks at 200 degrees C for about 12 minutes; turn them over and baste with the reserved marinade halfway through the cooking time.

Bon appétit!

Fish and Potato Croquettes

Prep time: 10 minutes / Cook time: 13 minutes / Serves 4 | Per Serving: Calories: 328 | Fat: 11.3g | Carbs: 42.3g | Fibre: 3.4g | Protein: 14.7g

Ingredients
- 300g catfish, skinless, boneless and chopped
- 2 potatoes, cooked and mashed
- 2 tbsp olive oil
- 2 cloves garlic, minced
- 1 small onion, minced
- 50g plain flour
- 50g breadcrumbs
- Sea salt and ground black pepper, to taste

Instructions
1. Mix all the Ingredients in a bowl. Shape the mixture into bite-sized balls and place them in a lightly greased cooking basket.
2. Cook the fish croquettes at 200 degrees C for about 13 minutes, shaking the basket halfway through the cooking time.

Bon appétit!

Roasted Tuna with Olives

Prep time: 10 minutes / Cook time: 11 minutes / Serves 4 | Per Serving: Calories: 272 | Fat: 15.7g | Carbs: 2.4g | Fibre: 0.8g | Protein: 30.3g

Ingredients
- 500g tuna steaks
- Sea salt and ground black pepper, to taste
- 1 tsp dried parsley flakes
- 1 tbsp olive oil
- 50g black olives, stoned and sliced
- 25g pine nuts, chopped

Instructions
1. Toss the tuna steaks with salt, pepper, parsley, and olive oil; place them in a lightly greased cooking basket.
2. Cook tuna steaks at 200 degrees C for about 6 minutes. Turn them over and continue to cook for a further 5 minutes.
3. Serve with black olives and pine nuts scattered over. Bon appétit!

Lime Crusted Fish Fillets

Prep time: 10 minutes / Cook time: 13 minutes / Serves 4 | Per Serving: Calories: 223 | Fat: 6.3g | Carbs: 13.7g | Fibre: 1g | Protein: 27.5g

Ingredients
- 500g tilapia fillets
- 2 tsp fresh lime juice
- 1 tbsp olive oil
- 100g bread crumbs
- 1 tsp red pepper flakes, crushed
- 1 tsp garlic granules
- Coarse sea salt and ground black pepper, to taste

Instructions
1. Toss the fish fillets with the other ingredients.
2. Lower them into a lightly greased Air Fryer cooking basket.
3. Air fry the fish fillets at 200 degrees C for 13 minutes. Bon appétit!

Prawn Katsu

Prep time: 10 minutes / Cook time: 11 minutes / Serves 4   Per Serving: Calories: 229 | Fat: 6g | Carbs: 16.9g | Fibre: 0.9g | Protein: 25.5g

Ingredients
- 500g tiger prawns, peeled, deveined, and rinsed well
- 1 shallot, quartered
- 1 egg white
- 2 tbsp cornflour
- 100g panko breadcrumbs
- 1 tbsp Cajun spice mix
- 1 tbsp olive oil

Instructions
1. Pat your prawns dry on kitchen paper.
2. Add all the ingredients, except the breadcrumbs, to a bowl of your food processor. Then, pulse to roughly chop them into the mixture.
3. Tip the breadcrumbs onto a plate. Shape the prawn mixture into burgers. Press the burgers into the crumbs, until they are coated on all sides.
4. Lower your prawns into the lightly greased basket. Drizzle the olive oil over the prawns.
5. Cook the prawns at 200 degrees C for about 11 minutes, shaking the basket halfway through the cooking time.

Enjoy!

Salmon and Asparagus Traybake

Prep time: 10 minutes / Cook time: 12 minutes / Serves 2   Per Serving: Calories: 354 | Fat: 22.8g | Carbs: 8.2g | Fibre: 3.2g | Protein: 29.5g

Ingredients
- 250g salmon fillets
- 250g asparagus spears, trimmed
- Sea salt and ground black pepper, to taste
- 2 tbsp olive oil
- 2 fat garlic cloves, minced
- 1 tbsp capers, plus extra to serve

Instructions
1. Toss the salmon and asparagus with the remaining Ingredients until they are well coated on all sides; place the salmon fillets in a lightly greased baking tray.
2. Roast the salmon fillets at 200 degrees C for about 4 minutes. Turn them over and add the asparagus spears.
3. Continue to cook for a further 8 minutes.
4. Serve with a salad on the side, if you like. Bon appétit!

Lemon & Pepper Fish

Prep time: 10 minutes / Cook time: 12 minutes / Serves 4

Per Serving: Calories: 165 | Fat: 4.3g | Carbs: 1.4g | Fibre: 0.3g | Protein: 28.3g

Ingredients
- 700g haddock fillets
- 1 tbsp olive oil
- 1/2 lemon, freshly squeezed
- 1/2 tsp cayenne pepper
- 1 tsp garlic granules
- 1 tsp black peppercorns, crushed
- Sea salt, to taste

Instructions
1. Toss haddock fillets with oil, lemon juice, and spices; place them in a lightly greased cooking basket.
2. Cook your fish at 200 degrees C for 7 minutes.
3. Turnt the fish fillets over and continue to cook for a further 5 minutes, or until the fish flakes when gently pressed.

Bon appétit!

Nutty Crusted Fish

Prep time: 10 minutes / Cook time: 13 minutes / Serves 2

Per Serving: Calories: 373 | Fat: 16.6g | Carbs: 31g | Fibre: 3.6g | Protein: 25.5g

Ingredients
- 2 (180g) cod fish fillets
- 2 tsp fresh lime juice
- 100g bread crumbs
- 30g almonds, chopped
- 1 tbsp groundnut oil
- 1 tsp red pepper flakes, crushed
- 1 tsp garlic granules
- Coarse sea salt and ground black pepper, to taste

Instructions
1. Toss the fish fillets with the other ingredients.
2. Lower them into a lightly oiled Air Fryer cooking basket.
3. Cook the fish fillets at 200 degrees C for 13 minutes. At the half point, turn the fish fillets over to promote even cooking.

Bon appétit!

5
BEANS & GRAINS

Bourbon Bread Pudding

Prep time: 10 minutes / Cook time: 20 minutes / Serves 5
Per Serving: Calories: 494 | Fat: 13.6g | Carbs: 79.1g | Fibre: 3.7g | Protein: 14g

Ingredients
- 1 loaf ciabatta bread, cubed
- 2 small eggs, whisked
- 100ml double cream
- 100ml whole milk
- 1/2 tsp vanilla essence
- 1 tbsp bourbon
- 50ml honey
- 60g golden raisins

Instructions
1. Place the ciabatta bread in a lightly greased baking tin (or casserole dish).
2. In a mixing bowl, thoroughly combine the eggs, double cream, milk, vanilla, bourbon, and honey.
3. Pour the cream mixture over the bread cubes. Fold in the raisins and set aside for 15 minutes to soak; press the top with a spatula.
4. Bake your bread pudding at 170 degrees C for about 20 minutes or until the custard is set but still a little wobbly.

Bon appétit!

Cheddar Cornbread Mini Loaves

Prep time: 10 minutes / Cook time: 22 minutes / Serves 9
Per Serving: Calories: 264 | Fat: 21.6g | Carbs: 12.1g | Fibre: 0.3g | Protein: 5.4g

Ingredients
- 70g strong white bread flour
- 150g polenta, instant
- 1 tbsp baking powder
- 100g butter, melted
- 2 large eggs
- 170 double cream
- 170ml whole milk
- 100g mature cheddar, grated

Instructions
1. Start by preheating your Air Fryer to 180 degrees C.
2. Mix all the Ingredients until everything is well incorporated. Scrape the batter into muffin cases and lower them into the Air Fryer basket.
3. Cover the top loosely with foil; otherwise, it will start to get dark too quickly.
4. Bake your mini cornbread loaves for about 22 minutes or until a tester comes out dry and clean. Work in batches, if needed.
5. Allow your mini cornbread loaves to cool before unmolding and serving. Bon appétit!

Prawn Wontons

Prep time: 10 minutes / Cook time: 15 minutes / Serves 10 | Per Serving: Calories: 260 | Fat: 4.6g | Carbs: 43.8g | Fibre: 2.3g | Protein: 10.4g

Ingredients
- 2 tbsp sesame oil
- 2 garlic cloves, crushed
- 2 tsp grated ginger purée
- 200g peeled prawn, finely chopped
- 2 spring onions, chopped small
- 200g cabbage, shredded
- 2 tbsp oyster sauce
- 5 water chestnuts, canned, drained and chopped
- 20 wonton wrappers, 9cm square, (thawed if frozen)

Instructions
1. Heat 1 tablespoon of sesame oil in a wok over medium-high heat; cook the garlic and ginger purée for about 30 seconds.
2. Then, sauté the prawn, onion, and cabbage for approximately 5 minutes.
3. Remove from the heat. Add in the oyster sauce and chestnuts; stir to combine well.
4. Peel off wonton wrappers and lightly brush around the outside with cold water
5. Divide the filling between wonton wrappers, squeezing to seal; do not overfill.
6. Lower the wonton wrappers into the Air Fryer cooking basket; do not overcrowd the basket. Brush your wontons with the remaining 1 tablespoon of sesame oil.
7. Cook the wonton wrappers at 185 degrees C for 9 to 10 minutes or to your desired level of crisp. Bon appétit!

Chorizo Tomato Pilaf

Prep time: 10 minutes / Cook time: 22 minutes / Serves 5 | Per Serving: Calories: 466 | Fat: 22.4g | Carbs: 48g | Fibre: 3.7g | Protein: 16.6g

Ingredients
- 250g basmati rice
- 600ml stock
- 1 tbsp olive oil
- 1 large onion, thinly sliced
- 4 garlic cloves, crushed
- 1 tsp smoked paprika
- 400g can chopped tomato
- 250g baby cooking chorizo, sliced
- 1 tbsp fresh parsley, chopped

Instructions
1. Start by preheating your Air Fryer to 180 degrees C.
2. Cook basmati rice with stock according to the package Instructions; it will take about 12 minutes
3. Add the rice and the other Ingredients to a lightly greased baking pan.
4. Lower the pan into the Air Fryer cooking basket. Cook your pilaf for about 10 minutes or until cooked through.

Bon appétit!

Baked Bhajis

Prep time: 10 minutes / Cook time: 20 minutes / Serves 6

Per Serving: Calories: 156 | Fat: 4.4g | Carbs: 20.7g | Fibre: 4.3g | Protein: 7.6g

Ingredients
- 150g chickpea (gram) flour
- 150g corn kernels, canned and creamed
- 1 large egg
- 1 tbsp tomato purée
- 1 tbsp medium curry powder
- 1 tsp ground turmeric
- 1 tsp vegetable bouillon powder
- 1 medium carrot, grated
- 2 green onions, thinly sliced
- 2 tsp rapeseed oil

Instructions
1. Start by preheating your Air Fryer to 190 degrees C.
2. Mix all the Ingredients until everything is well combined. Oil a baking tray and spoon on 6 mounds of batter.
3. Cook your bhajis for about 20 minutes or until golden. Turn them over halfway through the cooking time. Work in batches, if needed.

Bon appétit!

Apple Muffins

Prep time: 10 minutes / Cook time: 20 minutes / Serves 6

Ingredients
- 100g rolled oats, plus extra for sprinkling
- 100g wholemeal flour
- 1 tsp bicarbonate of soda
- 80g golden syrup
- 1 large egg, beaten
- 150g apple sauce
- 30ml coconut oil
- 50ml natural yoghurt

Instructions
1. Very lightly butter 6 muffin cases.
2. In a bowl, thoroughly combine all the dry ingredients. In a separate bowl, whisk the liquid ingredients.
3. Slowly and gradually, add the liquid mixture to the dry ingredients. Spoon the batter into the prepared muffin cases. Place muffin cases in the cooking basket.
4. Bake your muffins at 170 degrees C for 20 minutes.
5. Let your muffins cool on a rack for about 10 minutes before unmolding.

Enjoy!

Arancini Balls

Prep time: 10 minutes / Cook time: 16 minutes / Serves 6 | Per Serving: Calories: 390 | Fat: 12.4g | Carbs: 52.1g | Fibre: 1.7g | Protein: 15.8g

Ingredients
- 350g risotto rice
- 150ml dry white wine
- 1.2l hot veg stock
- 150g parmesan, finely grated
- 1 tbsp olive oil
- 1 tbsp unsalted butter, melted
- 1 shallot, finely chopped
- 1 fat garlic clove, crushed
- 1 small lemon, finely zested

Instructions
1. Cook your rice with wine and stock until the liquid is completely absorbed. Fluff the rice with a fork.
2. Mix all the Ingredients until everything is well combined. Form the mixture into balls.
3. Air fry the arancini at 180 degrees C for 16 minutes or until cooked through. Shake the cooking basket halfway through the cooking time.

Bon appétit!

Easy Macaroni Cheese

ving: Calories: 413 | Fat: 16.3g | Carbs: 48g | Fibre: 1.7g | Protein: 17.3g

Ingredients
- 350g macaroni
- 30g unsalted butter
- 2 tbsp plain flour
- 250ml whole milk
- 200g mature cheddar, grated

Instructions
1. Boil macaroni according to the package Instructions.
2. Drain macaroni and place them in a lightly greased baking tray. Add in the butter, flour, and milk; stir to combine.
3. Bake your macaroni cheese in the preheated Air Fryer at 180 degrees C for about 16 minutes.
4. At the half point, top your macaroni with cheese and continue to cook until everything is cooked through.
5. Serve garnished with fresh Italian parsley, if desired.

Bon appétit!

Aromatic Coconut Oatmeal

Prep time: 10 minutes / Cook time: 20 minutes / Serves 5 — Per Serving: Calories: 304 | Fat: 7.7g | Carbs: 47.4g | Fibre: 6.6g | Protein: 11.6g

Ingredients
- 250g porridge oats
- 1 tbsp chia seeds
- 1 cup full-fat oat milk
- 1 large egg, beaten
- 100ml apple sauce
- 50ml agave syrup
- 1 tsp coconut oil
- 4 tbsp coconut shreds
- 1/4 tsp ground cinnamon
- A pinch of sea salt

Instructions
1. Brush the inside of a baking tin with coconut oil. Thoroughly combine all the ingredients; spoon the mixture into the prepared baking tin.
2. Bake your oatmeal at 180 degrees C for 20 minutes.
3. Divide your oatmeals between five serving bowls; garnish them with fruits and nuts, if desired. Enjoy!

Granola with Cranberries

Prep time: 10 minutes / Cook time: 15 minutes / Serves 9 — Per Serving: Calories: 472 | Fat: 23.3g | Carbs: 55.4g | Fibre: 8.4g | Protein: 15.6g

Ingredients
- 400g porridge oats
- 50ml coconut oil
- 80ml clear honey
- 1 tsp ground ginger
- 1/2 tsp ground cinnamon
- 1 tsp vanilla extract
- 50g pumpkin seeds
- 50g sunflower seeds
- 30g golden linseed
- A pinch of fine sea salt
- A pinch of ground cloves
- 100g flaked almonds
- 100g dried cranberries

Instructions
1. Start by preheating your Air Fryer to 160 degrees C.
2. Thoroughly combine all the Ingredients in a parchment-lined roasting tray.
3. Then, place the roasting tray in the Air Fryer cooking basket. Bake your granola for about 15 minutes, stirring every 5 minutes.
4. Store at room temperature in an airtight container for up to three weeks.

Bon appétit!

Oat Biscuits

Prep time: 10 minutes / Cook time: 15 minutes / Serves 5
Per Serving: Calories: 252 | Fat: 12.3g | Carbs: 30.4g | Fibre: 1.8g | Protein: 4.1g

Ingredients
- 70g porridge oats
- 70g wholemeal flour
- 1/2 tsp baking powder
- 1/2 tsp bicarbonate of soda
- 50g golden caster sugar
- 70g butter, melted
- 3 tbsp milk

Instructions
1. Start by preheating your Air Fryer to 180 degrees C.
2. Mix all the Ingredients until well combined. Use a biscuit cutter and cut out biscuits. Place the biscuits on a lightly greased baking pan.
3. Lower the pan into the cooking basket.
4. Bake your biscuits in the preheated Air Fryer for about 15 minutes or until a tester comes out dry.

Bon appétit!

Millet and Bean Croquettes

Prep time: 10 minutes / Cook time: 13 minutes / Serves 4
Per Serving: Calories: 338 | Fat: 9.3g | Carbs: 52.8g | Fibre: 5.7g | Protein: 9.5g

Ingredients
- 150g millet, soaked overnight
- 100g canned black beans
- 2 tbsp olive oil
- 2 fat cloves garlic, minced
- 1 shallot, minced
- 50g plain flour
- 50g breadcrumbs
- 1 tsp red pepper
- 1/2 tsp ground cumin
- Sea salt and ground black pepper, to taste

Instructions
1. Mix all the Ingredients in a bowl. Shape the mixture into bite-sized balls using oiled hands.
2. Place the balls in a lightly greased cooking basket.
3. Cook the croquettes at 200 degrees C for about 13 minutes, shaking the basket halfway through the cooking time.

Bon appétit!

Baked Beans with Chorizo

Prep time: 10 minutes / Cook time: 20 minutes / Serves 4 — Per Serving: Calories: 358 | Fat: 16.3g | Carbs: 35.4g | Fibre: 8.3g | Protein: 19.2g

Ingredients
- 1 tsp grapeseed oil
- 1 (400g) can white beans, drained
- 200ml tomato paste
- 1 medium onion, chopped
- 2 garlic cloves, minced
- 1 tsp bouillon powder
- 1/4 tsp cumin seeds, ground
- 1/4 tsp coriander seeds, ground
- 1 bay leaf
- 200g cooking chorizo sausages, sliced

Instructions
1. Brush the inside of a baking tin with oil. Add the beans, tomato paste, onions, garlic, bouillon powder, cumin, coriander, and bay leaf.
2. Fold in the sausages and place the baking tin in the cooking basket.
3. Bake your beans at 180 degrees C for about 20 minutes.

Bon appétit!

Mushroom and Bacon Risotto

Prep time: 20 minutes / Cook time: 25 minutes / Serves 5 — Per Serving: Calories: 488 | Fat: 12.4g | Carbs: 73.3g | Fibre: 5.5g | Protein: 21.4g

Ingredients
- 1.3l chicken stock
- 300g risotto rice (arborio works well)
- 100g dried porcini mushrooms
- 200g pack dessert chestnut mushrooms, sliced
- 4 rashers smoked streaky bacon, chopped
- 1 onion, finely chopped
- 100ml port wine
- 60g parmesan, finely grated
- A handful of parsley leaves, chopped

Instructions
1. Start by preheating your Air Fryer to 180 degrees C. Soak the dried mushrooms in 500ml boiling water; it will take about 20 minutes.
2. Cook the rice with stock according to the package Instructions; it will take about 15 minutes
3. Add the rice and the other Ingredients to a lightly greased baking pan.
4. Lower the pan into the Air Fryer cooking basket. Cook your risotto for about 10 minutes or until cooked through.

Bon appétit!

6
VEGAN & VEGETARIAN

Vegan Bean "Meatballs"

Prep time: 10 minutes / Cook time: 16 minutes / Serves 5
Per Serving: Calories: 299 | Fat: 7.4g | Carbs: 43.2g | Fibre: 4.7g | Protein: 10.8g

Ingredients
- 200g risotto rice
- 100ml dry white wine
- 1l hot veg stock
- 200g canned or boiled kidney beans, drained and rinsed
- 1 tbsp olive oil
- 1 shallot, finely chopped
- 1 fat garlic clove, crushed

Instructions
1. Cook your rice with wine and stock until the liquid is completely absorbed. Fluff the rice with a fork.
2. Mix all the Ingredients until everything is well combined in your blender. Shape the mixture into balls.
3. Air fry the balls at 180 degrees C for 16 minutes or until cooked through. Shake the cooking basket halfway through the cooking time.

Bon appétit!

Double Bean Vegetarian Chilli

Prep time: 10 minutes / Cook time: 20 minutes / Serves 5
Per Serving: Calories: 269 | Fat: 6.4g | Carbs: 42g | Fibre: 7.4g | Protein: 12.6g

Ingredients
- 2 tbsp olive oil
- 1 medium leek, chopped
- 1 small celery root, chopped
- 1 bell pepper, seeded and chopped
- 1 bay leaf
- 1 tsp chipotle paste
- 1 tbsp ground coriander
- 200g can tomatoes, crushed
- 1 (400g) can kidney beans, drained and rinsed
- 1 (400g) can refried beans

Instructions
1. Heat 1 tablespoon of oil in a frying pan over medium-high heat. Once hot, sauté the leek, celery, and pepper for about 4 minutes, until just tender.
2. Brush the inside of a baking tin with cooking oil. Thoroughly combine all the ingredients, including the sauteed vegetables.
3. Spoon the mixture into the baking tin and lower it into the cooking basket.
4. Bake your chilli at 180 degrees C for 20 minutes.

Bon appétit!

Cajun Lentil and Quinoa

Prep time: 5 minutes / Cook time: 23 minutes / Serves 4
Per Serving: Calories: 272 | Fat: 6.4g | Carbs: 42g | Fibre: 7.2g | Protein: 13g

Ingredients
- 1 tbsp olive oil
- 100g quinoa
- 600ml hot veg stock
- 50g prunes, stoned and sliced
- 1 (250g pouch) ready-to-eat Puy lentils
- 1 large bunch spring onions, chopped
- 1 small bunch coriander, chopped
- 1 tbsp Cajun seasoning

Instructions
1. Brush the inside of a baking tray with olive oil.
2. Tip the quinoa into a deep saucepan and pour in the stock; bring it to a boil. Reduce the heat to medium-low and leave to simmer for approximately 10 minutes, stirring continuously, until the quinoa is tender.
3. Mix the quinoa with the other Ingredients and spoon the mixture into the prepared baking tray.
4. Bake in the preheated Air Fryer at 180 degrees C for about 13 minutes, or until thoroughly cooked.

Bon appétit!

Courgette and Sweetcorn Fritters

Prep time: 5 minutes / Cook time: 18 minutes / Serves 4
Per Serving: Calories: 270 | Fat: 8.4g | Carbs: 37.2g | Fibre: 2.8g | Protein: 6.6g

Ingredients
- 100g courgette, grated and squeezed
- 150g can sweetcorn, drained
- 2 spring onions, finely chopped
- 1 tsp smoked paprika
- 100g self-raising flour
- 50g tortilla chips, crushed
- 1 large egg, beaten
- 2 tbsp sweet chilli sauce
- 1 tbsp vegetable oil

Instructions
1. Add all the Ingredients to a mixing bowl; mix until everything is well incorporated.
2. Spoon four burger-sized mounds of the fritter mixture into a parchment-lined cooking basket.
3. Air fry your fritters at 180 degrees C for 18 minutes or until cooked through.

Bon appétit!

Italian Mushroom Risotto

Prep time: 20 minutes / Cook time: 25 minutes / Serves 4 — Per Serving: Calories: 503 | Fat: 3.4g | Carbs: 94.3g | Fibre: 5.5g | Protein: 21.4g

Ingredients
- 1l chicken stock
- 200g arborio rice
- 100g dried porcini mushrooms
- 200g pack brown Italian mushrooms, sliced
- 1 onion, finely chopped
- 100ml Italian cooking wine
- 60g parmesan, finely grated
- A handful of parsley leaves, chopped

Instructions
1. Start by preheating your Air Fryer to 180 degrees C. Soak the dried mushrooms in 500ml boiling water; it will take about 20 minutes.
2. Cook the rice with stock according to the package Instructions; it will take about 15 minutes
3. Add the rice and the other Ingredients to a lightly greased baking pan.
4. Lower the pan into the Air Fryer cooking basket. Cook your risotto for about 10 minutes or until cooked through.

Bon appétit!

Paprika Parmesan Sweet Potatoes

Prep time: 10 minutes / Cook time: 40 minutes / Serves 4 — Per Serving: Calories: 253 | Fat: 13.4g | Carbs: 23.3g | Fibre: 2.7g | Protein: 9.5g

Ingredients
- 2 medium sweet potatoes, scrubbed and halved
- 2 tbsp olive oil
- 1 tsp hot paprika
- Sea salt and ground black pepper, to taste
- 100g parmesan cheese, grated

Instructions
1. Toss sweet potatoes with the olive oil, paprika, salt, and black pepper.
2. Cook sweet potatoes at 200 degrees C for 30 minutes.
3. Top sweet potatoes with cheese and continue to bake for a further 10 minutes.
4. Taste and adjust the seasonings. Bon appétit!

Green Bean and Tofu Salad

Prep time: 10 minutes / Cook time: 20 minutes / Serves 4 Per Serving: Calories: 215 | Fat: 11.4g | Carbs: 23g | Fibre: 8g | Protein: 11.7g

Ingredients
- 160g tofu
- 2 tbsp cornflour
- 300g fresh green beans, washed and trimmed
- 2 tbsp extra-virgin olive oil
- 2 green onions, thinly sliced
- 1 large tomato, diced
- 1 tbsp fresh basil, chopped
- 2 tbsp fresh lemon juice
- 1/2 tsp red pepper flakes, crushed
- Sea salt and ground black pepper, to taste

Instructions
1. Drain the tofu; then, wrap it in 4 sheets of kitchen paper. Now, put something heavy over the top (a wooden chopping board will work well).
2. Leave for 20 minutes to drain the excess moisture from your tofu. Then, cut your tofu into cubes and toss them in the cornflour to coat all over.
3. Toss the green beans with 1 tablespoon of olive oil, salt, and black pepper. Arrange the green beans in the cooking basket.
4. Cook green beans at 190 degrees F for 10 minutes; add tofu cubes and continue to cook for a further 10 minutes.
5. Add the green beans to a salad bowl; add in the remaining Ingredients and stir to combine well. Enjoy!

Baked Breaded Mushrooms

Prep time: 10 minutes / Cook time: 15 minutes / Serves 2 Per Serving: Calories: 305 | Fat: 2.6g | Carbs: 51.3g | Fibre: 8.3g | Protein: 10.7g

Ingredients
- 200g chestnut mushrooms, halved
- 50g flour
- 1 medium egg, whisked
- 100g breadcrumbs
- 1 tsp smoked paprika
- Sea salt and ground black pepper, to taste

Instructions
1. Pat the mushrooms dry with tea towels. Trim the mushroom stalks level with their caps.
2. Place the flour on a plate. Whisk the egg in a shallow bowl. In the third bowl, mix the breadcrumbs, paprika, salt, and black pepper.
3. Dip your mushrooms in the flour, then in the whisked egg; finally, toss them in the breadcrumb mixture. Toss until they are well coated on all sides.
4. Cook the mushrooms at 190 degrees F for about 15 minutes, turning them halfway through the cooking time.

Bon appétit!

BBQ Tempeh Salad

Prep time: 10 minutes / Cook time: 15 minutes / Serves 4 | Per Serving: Calories: 333 | Fat: 21.3g | Carbs: 16.7g | Fibre: 1.3g | Protein: 24.4g

Ingredients
- 500g tempeh, pressed and cubed
- 1 tbsp soy sauce
- 1 tsp red pepper flakes, crushed
- 30ml BBQ sauce
- 100g cherry tomatoes, halved
- 2 handfuls Romaine lettuce, shredded
- 1 small onion, thinly sliced
- 2 tbsp extra-virgin olive oil
- 2 tbsp fresh lemon juice

Instructions
1. Cut your tempeh into bite-sized cubes and toss them with soy sauce, red pepper flakes, and BBQ sauce.
2. Cook your tempeh at 190 degrees C for about 10 minutes; turn them over and cook for a further 5 minutes.
3. In a salad bowl, toss the tempeh cubes with the remaining Ingredients and serve immediately.

Bon appétit!

Grilled Stuffed Aubergine Rolls

Prep time: 10 minutes / Cook time: 10 minutes / Serves 2 | Per Serving: Calories: 193 | Fat: 4.3g | Carbs: 34.7g | Fibre: 13g | Protein: 7.7g

Ingredients
- 1 medium aubergine
- 1 tsp olive oil
- 100g canned or boiled chickpeas, rinsed and drained
- 100g roasted peppers in a jar, chopped
- Sea salt and ground black pepper, to taste
- 1/2 tsp ground coriander seeds
- 1/2 tsp cayenne pepper

Instructions
1. Trim the aubergines and slice lengthwise into 1/2cm-thick slices and toss them with olive oil. Arrange them on the lightly greased cooking basket in a single layer.
2. Cook the aubergine slices at 200 degrees C for about 10 minutes; cook the aubergine in batches, if needed.
3. Meanwhile, mash canned chickpeas with roasted peppers, salt, black pepper, cayenne pepper, and ground coriander.
4. Top the aubergine slices with the chickpea mixture; roll them up and serve immediately. Enjoy!

Barbecued Vegan "Chicken"

Prep time: 10 minutes / Cook time: 13 minutes / Serves 4 | Per Serving: Calories: 139 | Fat: 4.3g | Carbs: 7.7g | Fibre: 2.6g | Protein: 21.7g

Ingredients
- 100g soy curls
- 100ml hot water
- 100ml passata
- 1 tsp onion flakes
- 1 tsp dried parsley flakes
- 1/2 tsp garlic granules
- 1/2 tsp chilli pepper flakes
- 1 tbsp olive oil

Instructions
1. Soak soy curls in hot water for approximately 10 minutes. Drain the soy curls in a mesh sieve, squeezing out all excess liquid.
2. Toss the soy curls with the remaining Ingredients and place them in the lightly greased cooking basket.
3. Cook the soy curls at 180 degrees C for approximately 13 minutes, until thoroughly cooked.

Bon appétit!

Quinoa and Chickpea Patties

Prep time: 10 minutes / Cook time: 18 minutes / Serves 4 | Per Serving: Calories: 319 | Fat: 7g | Carbs: 50.3g | Fibre: 7.1g | Protein: 11.8g

Ingredients
- 200g quinoa, soaked overnight
- 200g canned or boiled chickpeas, drained and rinsed
- 50g breadcrumbs
- 2 tsp olive oil
- 1 shallot, finely chopped
- 1 fat garlic clove, crushed

Instructions
1. Cook your rice with wine and stock until the liquid is completely absorbed. Fluff the rice with a fork.
2. Mix all the Ingredients until everything is well combined in your blender. Shape the mixture into patties.
3. Air fry the patties at 180 degrees C for 18 minutes or until cooked through. Shake the cooking basket halfway through the cooking time.

Bon appétit!

Vegan Burritos

Prep time: 30 minutes / Cook time: 19 minutes / Serves 4 | Per Serving: Calories: 309 | Fat: 17g | Carbs: 31.3g | Fibre: 6.1g | Protein: 12.1g

Ingredients
- 160g block tofu
- 2 tbsp vegan mayonnaise
- Ground black pepper, to taste
- 1 tsp garlic granules
- 1/2 tsp paprika
- 4 small tortillas
- 1 medium tomato, sliced
- 1 small avocado, peeled, pitted, and spiced
- 100g rocket lettuce

Instructions
1. Press your tofu: Place the folded paper towels on a working surface. Place the block of tofu on the paper towels.
2. Top the tofu with another layer of paper towels. Press it with a heavy pan or a wooden board. Allow your tofu to stand for at least 30 minutes.
3. Cut your tofu into 4 slices and toss them with mayonnaise, black pepper, garlic, and paprika.
4. Cook your tofu in the preheated Air Fryer at 200 degrees C for 15 minutes, until cooked through.
5. Warm tortillas at 160 degrees C for approximately 4 minutes. Lay out the tortillas and assemble them with tofu, tomato, avocado, and lettuce. Enjoy!

7
LIGHT BITES & SIDE DISHES

Burnt Butter Cabbage

Prep time: 10 minutes / Cook time: 15 minutes / Serves 4   Per Serving: Calories: 124 | Fat: 6.4g | Carbs: 17.3g | Fibre: 4.8g | Protein: 3.4g

Ingredients
- 1 medium pointed cabbage, cleaned
- 2 tbsp butter, melted
- 1 garlic clove, minced
- 1 tsp hot paprika
- 1 tsp ginger root, peeled and grated
- Sea salt and ground black pepper, to taste

Instructions
1. Begin by preheating your Air Fryer to 190 degrees C.
2. Remove the outer leaves of the cabbage and cut it into eight wedges.
3. Toss the cabbage wedges with the other Ingredients and transfer them to the cooking basket.
4. Air fry the cabbage wedges in the preheated Air Fryer for about 15 minutes, until crisp-tender. Enjoy!

Paprika Okra Chips

Prep time: 10 minutes / Cook time: 20 minutes / Serves 4   Per Serving: Calories: 119 | Fat: 4g | Carbs: 19g | Fibre: 4.1g | Protein: 3.4g

Ingredients
- 400g okra, trimmed, washed, and sliced into halves
- 1 tbsp extra-virgin olive oil
- 50g cornmeal
- 1 tsp paprika
- 1/2 tsp ground coriander
- 1/2 tsp turmeric powder
- Sea salt and ground black pepper, to taste

Instructions
1. Toss okra halves with the other Ingredients until they are well coated on all sides.
2. Cook your okra in the preheated Air Fryer at 180 degrees C for about 20 minutes, shaking the basket once or twice to ensure even cooking.

Bon appétit!

Potato Rösti

Prep time: 10 minutes / Cook time: 25 minutes / Serves 4

Per Serving: Calories: 155 | Fat: 4.6g | Carbs: 23.4g | Fibre: 2.9g | Protein: 3.9g

Ingredients
- 500g Maris Piper potatoes, peeled and coarsely grated
- 1 small egg, beaten
- 1 tbsp plain flour
- 1/2 tsp baking powder
- 2 green onions, sliced
- 1 tbsp sunflower oil

Instructions
1. Coarsely grate your potatoes; wring out the liquid with a clean tea towel.
2. Add the other Ingredients to the grated potatoes. Brush the bottom of the cooking basket with nonstick cooking oil.
3. Shape the mixture into patties, flattening them down with the back of a spoon into disc shapes.
4. Cook your rosti at 190 degrees C for about 13 minutes. Turn them over and cook for a further 12 minutes, until thoroughly cooked.

Bon appétit!

Cheese Stuffed Mushrooms

Prep time: 10 minutes / Cook time: 13 minutes / Serves 4

Per Serving: Calories: 195 | Fat: 12.6g | Carbs: 12g | Fibre: 1.8g | Protein: 9.3g

Ingredients
- 4 portobello mushrooms
- 1 tbsp olive oil
- Sea salt and ground black pepper, to your liking
- 1/2 tsp dried rosemary
- 1/2 tsp red pepper flakes
- 1 red chilli pepper, seeded and chopped
- 50g breadcrumbs
- 100g sharp cheddar cheese, preferably freshly grated

Instructions
1. Remove the stems from the mushroom caps; chop the stems and reserve.
2. In a mixing bowl, thoroughly combine the remaining ingredients, including the reserved mushroom stems; divide the filling among the mushroom caps.
3. Cook the stuffed mushrooms in the preheated Air Fryer at 190 degrees for about 13 minutes.

Bon appétit!

Cajun King Prawn

Prep time: 10 minutes / Cook time: 11 minutes / Serves 4

Per Serving: Calories: 212 | Fat: 6g | Carbs: 16.1g | Fibre: 0.7g | Protein: 21.5g

Ingredients
- 500g king prawns, peeled and deveined
- 280ml tub buttermilk
- 200g corn flour
- Sea salt and ground black pepper, to taste
- 1 tbsp Cajun spice mix
- 1 tbsp olive oil

Instructions
1. Decant the buttermilk into a bowl and give it a good stir. In another bowl, mix the corn flour, salt, pepper, and Cajun spice mix.
2. Dip each prawn in the buttermilk then coat in the flour mixture.
3. Arrange your prawns in the Air Fryer basket. Drizzle the olive oil over the prawns.
4. Cook the prawns at 200 degrees C for about 11 minutes, shaking the basket halfway through the cooking time.
5. Serve with toothpicks and enjoy!

Red Beet Salad

Prep time: 10 minutes / Cook time: 40 minutes / Serves 4

Per Serving: Calories: 212 | Fat: 6g | Carbs: 16.1g | Fibre: 0.7g | Protein: 21.5g

Ingredients
- 500g red beets, peeled
- 2 tbsp extra-virgin olive oil
- 1 tbsp fresh lemon juice
- 1 tbsp apple cider vinegar
- 1 tsp English mustard
- 1 garlic clove, minced
- 1/2 tsp cumin, ground
- Sea salt and ground black pepper, to taste
- 1/2 small bunch parsley, roughly chopped

Instructions
1. Place the beets in a single layer in the lightly greased cooking basket.
2. Cook the beets at 200 degrees C for 40 minutes, shaking the basket halfway through the cooking time.
3. Let the beets cool and cut them into slices; then, toss the beet slices with the remaining ingredients.
4. Place the salad in the fridge until ready to serve.

Enjoy!

Spicy Sweet Potato Chips

Prep time: 20 minutes / Cook time: 20 minutes / Serves 4   Per Serving: Calories: 162 | Fat: 3.6g | Carbs: 30.6g | Fibre: 4.6g | Protein: 2.5g

Ingredients
- 600g sweet potatoes, peeled
- 1 tbsp olive oil
- 1 tsp chilli powder
- 1 tsp garlic granules
- Coarse sea salt and freshly ground black pepper, to taste

Instructions
1. Cut sweet potatoes into 1/2 cm thick slices. Place sweet potato slices in a bowl of cold water; let sweet potatoes sit for about 20 minutes.
2. Toss sweet potato slices with the remaining ingredients.
3. Cook sweet potato chips in the preheated Air Fryer at 180 degrees C for about 10 minutes; shake the cooking basket and cook for a further 10 minutes.
4. Serve sweet potato chips with the sauce for dipping, if desired. Enjoy!

Butternut Squash Mash

Prep time: 10 minutes / Cook time: 20 minutes / Serves 4   Per Serving: Calories: 97 | Fat: 3.1g | Carbs: 18.6g | Fibre: 4.6g | Protein: 3.4g

Ingredients
- 600g butternut squash, peeled
- 1 tbsp butter, unsalted
- 1 tsp paprika
- 1/2 tsp ground cinnamon
- 1 tsp garlic granules
- A small handful of fresh parsley leaves, roughly chopped

Instructions
1. Start by preheating your Air Fryer to 195 degrees C. Cut the butternut squash into small wedges. Toss the butternut squash with the butter, paprika, cinnamon, and garlic granules.
2. Roast the butternut squash in the preheated Air Fryer for 10 minutes. Shake the basket and continue to cook for 10 minutes longer.
3. Purée the butternut squash using an immersion blender or potato masher. Garnish butternut squash mash with fresh parsley leaves.

Bon appétit!

Cauliflower Fritters

Prep time: 10 minutes / Cook time: 13 minutes / Serves 4 Per Serving: Calories: 230 | Fat: 5.4g | Carbs: 37.3g | Fibre: 4.1g | Protein: 7.1g

Ingredients
- 350g cauliflower, grated
- 1 small carrot, grated
- 2 garlic cloves, finely chopped
- 1 small leek, finely chopped
- 60ml soy milk
- 50g plain flour
- 100g dried breadcrumbs
- 1 tbsp olive oil

Instructions
1. In a mixing bowl, thoroughly combine the vegetables, soy milk, and flour; mix until everything is well incorporated.
2. Shape the mixture into small balls; slightly flatten them with a fork. Place the breadcrumbs on a plate.
3. Roll the balls into the breadcrumbs and brush them with olive oil.
4. Air fry the cauliflower croquettes in the preheated Air Fryer at 190 degrees C for 7 minutes. Turn them over and cook for a further 6 minutes.
5. Serve warm and enjoy!

Bacon-Wrapped Scallops

Prep time: 10 minutes / Cook time: 8 minutes / Serves 6 Per Serving: Calories: 223 | Fat: 15.4g | Carbs: 5.4g | Fibre: 0.2g | Protein: 15.1g

Ingredients
- 6 scallops
- Sea salt and ground black pepper, to taste
- 1 tsp red pepper flakes, crushed
- 1 tbsp English mustard
- 1 tsp honey
- 2 tbsp olive oil
- 1 tbsp lemon juice, freshly squeezed
- 6 thin rashers streaky bacon

Instructions
1. Spray the cooking basket with cooking oil.
2. Toss your scallops with salt, black pepper, red pepper flakes, mustard, and honey; drizzle the scallops with olive oil and lemon juice.
3. Wrap one rasher of bacon around each scallop; secure with toothpicks. Arrange the bacon-wrapped scallops in the prepared cooking basket.
4. Cook the scallops at 200 degrees C for approximately 8 minutes. After 4 minutes, turn the bacon-wrapped scallops over using silicone-tipped tongs. Enjoy!

Crunchy Popcorn Chicken

Prep time: 30 minutes / Cook time: 18 minutes / Serves 6   Per Serving: Calories: 306 | Fat: 10.4g | Carbs: 26.4g | Fibre: 1.4g | Protein: 25.1g

Ingredients
- 600g chicken breasts, skinless, boneless, cut into bite-sized pieces
- 100g plain flour
- 2 tbsp buttermilk
- 150g fresh breadcrumb
- 1 tsp paprika
- 1/2 tsp garlic granules
- 1/2 tsp cumin seeds
- Sea salt and ground black pepper, to taste
- 1 tbsp olive oil

Instructions
1. Pat the chicken pieces dry with tea towels.
2. Add the plain flour to a shallow dish. Add buttermilk to a second shallow dish.
3. Tip the breadcrumbs and spices into a third shallow dish.
4. Dip the chicken pieces into the flour, then into the buttermilk. Lastly, roll the chicken pieces into the breadcrumb mixture.
5. Place the chicken pieces in the fridge for approximately 30 minutes, until well-chilled. Then, transfer the chicken pieces to the cooking basket. Brush them with olive oil.
6. Air fry popcorn chicken at 200 degrees C for 18 minutes, turning them over once or twice to promote even cooking.

Bon appétit!

8
DESSERTS

Chocolate Brownies

Prep time: 10 minutes / Cook time: 20 minutes / Serves 9 | Per Serving: Calories: 433 | Fat: 21.4g | Carbs: 55.4g | Fibre: 3.3g | Protein: 5.7g

Ingredients
- 180g unsalted butter
- 270g golden caster sugar
- 3 medium eggs
- 200g best dark chocolate
- 80g plain flour
- 30g cocoa powder

Instructions
1. Start by preheating your Air Fryer to 170 degrees C. Now, spritz the sides and bottom of a baking tin with cooking spray.
2. In a mixing bowl, beat the melted butter and sugar until fluffy. Next, fold in the eggs and beat again until well combined.
3. After that, add the remaining ingredients. Mix until everything is well incorporated.
4. Bake your brownies in the preheated Air Fryer for 20 minutes. Enjoy!

Caramelized Plums

Prep time: 10 minutes / Cook time: 16 minutes / Serves 5 | Per Serving: Calories: 118 | Fat: 5.4g | Carbs: 18g | Fibre: 1.3g | Protein: 0.5g

Ingredients
- 350g plums, halved and stoned
- 2 tbsp coconut oil
- 4 tbsp brown sugar
- 1/4 tsp grated nutmeg
- 1/2 tsp ground cinnamon

Instructions
1. Toss the plums with the remaining ingredients.
2. Place the plum halves in the cooking basket.
3. Bake the plums at 170 degrees F for 16 minutes.

Bon appétit!

Banana Mug Cake

Prep time: 5 minutes / Cook time: 9 minutes / Serves 1 | Per Serving: Calories: 530 | Fat: 18.4g | Carbs: 86g | Fibre: 4.4g | Protein: 10g

Ingredients
- 1 banana, peeled
- 1 medium egg, beaten
- 1 tbsp coconut oil
- 1/2 tsp cinnamon powder
- 1/2 tsp vanilla extract
- 3 tbsp agave syrup
- 4 tbsp plain flour
- 1/2 tsp baking powder

Instructions
1. Tip the mashed banana into a microwave-safe mug.
2. Now, stir in the remaining ingredients.
3. Cook your mug cake at 180 degrees C for about 9 minutes. Devour!

Plum Flapjack Crumble

Prep time: 10 minutes / Cook time: 35 minutes / Serves 6 | Per Serving: Calories: 259 | Fat: 13.4g | Carbs: 34.8g | Fibre: 4.9g | Protein: 4.7g

Ingredients

- 200g plums, pitted and halved
- 1 small orange, zested and juiced
- 50g golden caster sugar

Topping:

- 120g porridge oats
- 50g brown sugar
- 50g coconut oil, melted
- 50ml dark rum
- 1/2 tsp ground cinnamon
- 100g pecans, chopped

Instructions
1. Toss your plums with orange and sugar. Arrange them in a lightly greased baking tray.
2. In a mixing dish, thoroughly combine all the topping ingredients. Sprinkle the topping Ingredients over the fruit layer. Place the baking tray in the cooking basket.
3. Bake your crumble in the preheated Air Fryer at 165 degrees C for 35 minutes. Let it cool for 10 minutes before serving.
4. Serve with custard, if desired. Bon appétit!

Peanut Butter Cookies

Prep time: 10 minutes / Cook time: 12 minutes / Serves 8 | Per Serving: Calories: 109 | Fat: 3g | Carbs: 18.5g | Fibre: 0.5g | Protein: 1.7g

Ingredients
- 120g peanut butter
- 1/2 tsp pure almond extract
- 1 tsp cinnamon powder
- 120g golden caster sugar
- A pinch of flaky sea salt
- 1/2 tsp bicarbonate of soda
- 1 small egg

Instructions
1. Begin by preheating your Air Fryer to 175 degrees C.
2. In a mixing bowl, beat the peanut butter, almond extract, cinnamon, sugar, salt, and bicarbonate of soda.
3. Mix until creamy and uniform. Now, fold in the egg and beat again until the mixture forms a dough.
4. Create small scoops of the dough, and arrange them on a cookie tin.
5. Bake your cookies in the preheated Air Fryer for 12 minutes, until golden around the edges.
6. Serve and enjoy!

Cinnamon Apple Fritters

Prep time: 10 minutes / Cook time: 13 minutes / Serves 4 | Per Serving: Calories: 319 | Fat: 6.3g | Carbs: 60.5g | Fibre: 3.8g | Protein: 6.7g

Ingredients
- 250g English apple, peeled
- 100g oat flour
- 50g plain flour
- 100g granulated sugar
- A pinch of sea salt
- 1 tsp cinnamon powder
- 1/2 tsp baking powder
- 50ml cup full-fat milk
- 1 medium egg, beaten
- 2 tsp coconut oil, melted

Instructions
1. Slice the apples into rings. Mix the flour, sugar, salt, cinnamon, and baking powder.
2. In a separate bowl, whisk the egg with milk; add this wet mixture to the dry ingredients; mix to combine well.
3. Dip apple rings into the batter; arrange them in the lightly greased cooking basket. Brush them with cooking oil.
4. Cook the apple fritters in the preheated Air Fryer at 185 degrees C for about 13 minutes, turning them over halfway through the cooking time.
5. Serve the apple fritters with vanilla ice cream, if used. Bon appétit!

Banana Muffins

Prep time: 10 minutes / Cook time: 20 minutes / Serves 6 — Per Serving: Calories: 155 | Fat: 2.1g | Carbs: 28.5g | Fibre: 3g | Protein: 6.3g

Ingredients
- 1 large egg
- 70ml pot natural yoghurt
- 30ml rapeseed oil
- 60g apple sauce or puréed apple
- 1 small ripe banana, mashed
- 2 tbsp honey
- 50g plain flour
- 100g rolled oats
- 1 tsp baking powder
- 1 tsp cinnamon, ground

Instructions
1. Start by preheating your Air Fryer to 175 degrees C. Brush a muffin tin (with 6 muffin cases) with cooking oil.
2. In a large mixing bowl, beat the egg until pale and frothy; gradually and carefully pour in the other liquid ingredients.
3. Gradually, stir in the dry ingredients. Stir with a wire whisk until a smooth batter forms. Do not overmix the batter.
4. Spoon the batter into the prepared muffin tin. Cook the muffins for approximately 20 minutes. Leave them to cool for 10 minutes before serving.

Bon appétit!

Chocolate Cupcakes

Prep time: 10 minutes / Cook time: 15 minutes / Serves 6 — Per Serving: Calories: 450 | Fat: 26.1g | Carbs: 46.5g | Fibre: 3.7g | Protein: 6.9g

Ingredients

- 150g dark chocolate, broken into chunks
- 100g self-raising flour
- 100g light muscovado sugar, plus 3 tbsp extra
- 3 tbsp cocoa
- 70ml sunflower oil, plus a little extra for greasing
- 140ml pot soured cream
- 1 small egg
- A pinch of grated nutmeg
- 1/2 tsp ground cinnamon
- 1 tsp vanilla extract

Instructions
1. Start by preheating your Air Fryer to 170 degrees C.
2. Mix all the Ingredients in a bowl. Scrape the batter into silicone muffin cases; place them in the cooking basket.
3. Bake your cupcakes for about 15 minutes or until a tester comes out dry and clean.
4. Allow the cupcakes to cool before unmolding. Bon appétit!

Bonus Recipe

Air-Fried English Muffins with

Serves 2 / Prep time: 5 minutes / Cook Time: 4 minutes Calories: 180 | Fat: 1g | Carbs: 40g | Fiber: 2g | Protein: 4g

- 2 English muffins (200g)
- Jam or preserves of your choice, for serving

Instructions
1. Preheat your air fryer to 350°F (175°C) for 5 minutes and split the English muffins in half.
2. Spray the air fryer basket with cooking spray or lightly oil it to prevent sticking.
3. Place the English muffin halves in the air fryer basket, cut side up.
4. Air fry the English muffins for 2 minutes at 350°F (175°C) until they are lightly toasted.
5. Remove the toasted English muffins from the air fryer and spread your favorite jam or preserves on top.

Air-Fried Bacon-Wrapped Asparagus Soldiers

Serves 2 / Prep time: 10 minutes / Cook Time: 10 minutes Calories: 280 | Fat: 20g | Carbs: 4g | Fiber: 2g | Protein: 20g

- 16 asparagus spears
- 8 slices of bacon
- Cooking spray or oil, for air frying
- Salt and pepper, to taste

Instructions
1. Preheat your air fryer to 400°F (200°C) for 5 minutes.
2. While the air fryer is preheating, trim the woody ends of the asparagus and season them with salt and pepper.
3. Take a slice of bacon and wrap it around an asparagus spear, repeating until all asparagus spears are wrapped.
4. Spray the air fryer basket with cooking spray or lightly oil it to prevent sticking.
5. Place the bacon-wrapped asparagus soldiers in the air fryer basket, ensuring they are not overlapping.
6. Air fry the asparagus for 10 minutes at 400°F (200°C) until the bacon is crispy and the asparagus is tender.

Air-Fried Baked Beans on Toast

Serves 2 / Prep time: 5 minutes / Cook Time: 5 minutes Calories: 320 | Fat: 1g | Carbs: 68g | Fiber: 14g | Protein: 14g

- 400g baked beans
- 2 slices of whole-grain bread
- Butter or margarine, for spreading (optional)

Instructions
1. Preheat your air fryer to 350°F (175°C) for 5 minutes.
2. As the air fryer is preheating, toast the slices of bread in the air fryer.
3. Optionally, spread butter or margarine on the toasted bread.
4. Pour the canned baked beans into an air fryer-safe dish that fits in your air fryer basket.
5. Place the dish with the baked beans in the air fryer basket.
6. Air fry the baked beans for 5 minutes at 350°F (175°C) until they are hot and bubbling.
7. Serve the hot baked beans over the toasted bread.

Air-Fried Kedgeree

Serves 2 / Prep time: 15 minutes / Cook Time: 20 minutes — Calories: 320 | Fat: 8g | Carbs: 34g | Fiber: 3g | Protein: 25g

- 200g smoked haddock or other white fish
- 150g cooked rice
- 2 large eggs
- 1 onion, finely chopped
- 1 tablespoon of vegetable oil
- 1 teaspoon of curry powder
- Salt and pepper, to taste
- Chopped fresh parsley, for garnish

Instructions

1. Preheat your air fryer to 375°F (190°C) for 5 minutes.
2. While the air fryer is preheating, place the smoked haddock in a microwave-safe dish, cover with a microwave-safe lid or microwave-safe plastic wrap, and microwave for 2 minutes on high power until it's just cooked through. Flake the fish into small pieces.
3. Boil the eggs for 8-10 minutes until hard-boiled, then peel and chop them.
4. In a skillet, heat the vegetable oil over medium heat. Add the chopped onion and cook for 2-3 minutes until softened.
5. Stir in the curry powder and cook for an additional minute.
6. Add the cooked rice, flaked smoked haddock, and chopped hard-boiled eggs to the skillet. Mix everything together and cook for another 2-3 minutes until heated through.
7. Spray the air fryer basket with cooking spray or lightly oil it to prevent sticking.
8. Transfer the kedgeree mixture to the air fryer basket.
9. Air fry the kedgeree for 10 minutes at 375°F (190°C), stirring occasionally to ensure even heating.
10. Garnish with chopped fresh parsley, if desired, before serving.

Air-Fried Cream Cheese Bagels

Serves 2 / Prep time: 5 minutes / Cook Time: 8 minutes — Calories: 420 | Fat: 26g | Carbs: 38g | Fiber: 2g | Protein: 8g

- 2 bagels, split
- 60g cream cheese
- 2 tablespoons butter
- Cooking spray or oil, for air frying

Instructions

1. Preheat your air fryer to 350°F (175°C) for 5 minutes.
2. While the air fryer is preheating, spread cream cheese on the inside of each bagel half.
3. Sandwich the bagel halves back together.
4. Lightly spread butter on the outside of each bagel.
5. Spray the air fryer basket with cooking spray or lightly oil it to prevent sticking.
6. Place the bagels in the air fryer basket.
7. Air fry the bagels for 4 minutes at 350°F (175°C), then flip them over.
8. Continue air frying for another 4 minutes until the bagels are toasted and crispy on the outside.

Air-Fried Lamb Chump

Serves 2 / Prep time: 10 minutes / Cook Time: 14 minutes
Calories: 400 | Fat: 30g | Carbs: 0g | Fiber: 0g | Protein: 30g

- 2 lamb chump chops (150g each)
- 1 tablespoon olive oil
- 2 cloves garlic, minced
- 1 teaspoon dried rosemary
- Salt and pepper, to taste

Instructions

1. Preheat your air fryer to 375°F (190°C) for 5 minutes.
2. Season the lamb chump chops with olive oil, minced garlic, dried rosemary, salt, and pepper.
3. Place the seasoned lamb chump chops in the air fryer basket.
4. Air fry the lamb chump chops for 12-14 minutes at 375°F (190°C) until they are cooked to your desired level of doneness.
5. Let the lamb chops rest for a few minutes before serving.

Turkey Crown with Cranberry Glaze

Serves 2/ Prep time: 15 minutes / Cook Time: 35 minutes
Calories: 400 | Fat: 12g | Carbs: 45g | Fiber: 2g | | Protein: 30g

- 500g turkey crown
- 15g olive oil
- Salt and pepper to taste
- 100g cranberry sauce
- 30g honey
- 15g orange juice
- 5g cornstarch
- 15g water

Instructions

1. Preheat your air fryer to 350°F (180°C).
2. Season the turkey crown with olive oil, salt, and pepper.
3. Place the turkey crown in the air fryer basket, breast side down.
4. Cook for 25 minutes.
5. While the turkey is cooking, prepare the cranberry glaze. In a small saucepan, combine cranberry sauce, honey, and orange juice.
6. In a separate bowl, mix cornstarch and water until smooth, then add it to the saucepan.
7. Cook the glaze over medium heat, stirring constantly, until it thickens.
8. After the initial 25 minutes of cooking, carefully flip the turkey crown and cook for an additional 10 minutes or until the internal temperature reaches 165°F (74°C).
9. Brush the turkey crown with the cranberry glaze during the last 5 minutes of cooking.
10. Once done, remove the turkey from the air fryer, let it rest for a few minutes, and then slice.

Air-Fried Lamb Chops with Rosemary and Mint Sauce

Serves 2/ Prep time: 10 minutes / Cook Time: 15 minutes
Calories: 350 | Fat: 20g | Carbs: 1g | Fiber: 0g | | Protein: 40g

- 400g lamb chops
- 10g olive oil
- Salt and pepper to taste
- 10g fresh rosemary, minced
- 10g fresh mint leaves, minced
- 15g lemon juice

Instructions
1. Preheat your air fryer to 375°F (190°C).
2. Rub the lamb chops with olive oil and season with salt, pepper, and minced rosemary.
3. Place the lamb chops in the air fryer basket.
4. Cook for 12-15 minutes, turning them halfway through the cooking time until they reach your desired level of doneness.
5. While the lamb chops are cooking, prepare the mint sauce. In a small bowl, mix together the minced mint leaves and lemon juice.
6. Once the lamb chops are done, remove them from the air fryer.
7. Drizzle the mint sauce over the lamb chops before serving.

Air-Fried Pork Loin with Apple Compote

Serves 2 / Prep time: 15 minutes / Cook Time: 25 minutes Calories: 300 | Fat: 10g | Carbs: 25g | Fiber: 4g | Protein: 30g

- 400g pork loin
- 10g olive oil
- Salt and pepper to taste
- 200g apples, peeled and diced
- 10g brown sugar
- 5g cinnamon
- 10g lemon juice

Instructions
1. Preheat your air fryer to 375°F (190°C).
2. Rub the pork loin with olive oil and season with salt and pepper.
3. Place the pork loin in the air fryer basket.
4. Cook for 20-25 minutes. Turn it halfway through the cooking time.
5. While the pork loin is cooking, prepare the apple compote. In a saucepan, combine the diced apples, brown sugar, cinnamon, and lemon juice.
6. Cook over medium heat, stirring occasionally, until the apples are soft and the mixture thickens.
7. Once the pork loin is done, remove it from the air fryer and let it rest for a few minutes before slicing.
8. Serve the sliced pork loin with the apple compote on top.

Lamb Shank with Red Wine Gravy

Serves 2 /Prep time: 20 minutes / Cook Time: 2 hours Calories: 550 | Fat: 30g | Carbs: 15g | Fiber: 2g | Protein: 45g

- For the Lamb Shank:
- 2 lamb shanks (350g each)
- Salt and pepper, to taste
- 2 tablespoons olive oil
- 150g onion, chopped
- 2 cloves garlic, minced
- 2 carrots, chopped
- 2 celery stalks, chopped
- 240ml red wine
- 480ml beef broth
- 1 teaspoon dried rosemary
- 1 teaspoon dried thyme
- For the Red Wine Gravy:
- 120ml red wine
- 1 tablespoon cornstarch

- Salt and pepper, to taste

Instructions
1. Preheat your air fryer to 375°F (190°C) for 5 minutes.
2. Season the lamb shanks with salt and pepper.
3. In a large skillet, heat the olive oil over medium-high heat. Sear the lamb shanks on all sides until browned. Remove from the skillet and set aside.
4. In the same skillet, add the chopped onion, minced garlic, chopped carrots, and chopped celery. Sauté until the vegetables are softened.
5. Return the seared lamb shanks to the skillet and add the red wine, beef broth, dried rosemary, and dried thyme.
6. Transfer the lamb shanks and liquid to an oven-safe dish that fits in your air fryer basket.
7. Air fry the lamb shanks at 375°F (190°C) for 1.5 to 2 hours, turning occasionally, until the meat is tender and easily pulls away from the bone.
8. While the lamb shanks are cooking, prepare the red wine gravy. In a saucepan, combine 1/2 cup of red wine and cornstarch. Cook over medium heat, stirring constantly, until the gravy thickens. Season with salt and pepper to taste.
9. Serve the air-fried lamb shanks with the red wine gravy.

Air-Fried Smoked Salmon and Cream Cheese Pinwheels

Serves 2 /Prep time: 15 minutes / Cook Time: 8 minutes   Calories: 200 | Fats: 15g | Carbs: 5g | Fiber: 1g | Protein: 10g

- 4 slices smoked salmon
- 60g cream cheese
- 25g red onion, finely chopped
- 2 tablespoons fresh dill, chopped
- 1 lemon, zested
- Salt and pepper, to taste

Instructions
1. Preheat your air fryer to 375°F (190°C) for 5 minutes.
2. In a bowl, combine the cream cheese, finely chopped red onion, chopped fresh dill, lemon zest, salt, and pepper. Mix until well combined.
3. Lay out the smoked salmon slices on a clean surface.
4. Spread the cream cheese mixture evenly over each slice of smoked salmon.
5. Carefully roll up each slice into a tight pinwheel.
6. Place the pinwheels in the air fryer basket.
7. Air fry the pinwheels for 6-8 minutes at 375°F (190°C) until they are heated through and slightly crispy on the outside.
8. Serve immediately.

Air-Fried Lobster Bisque

Serves 2 /Prep time: 15 minutes / Cook Time: 15 minutes   Calories: 450 | Fats: 30g | Carbs: 15g | Fiber: 2g | Protein: 20g

- 200g lobster meat, cooked and chopped
- 100g onion, finely chopped
- 10g garlic, minced
- 60g tomato paste
- 480ml fish or seafood broth
- 120ml heavy cream
- 2 tablespoons butter
- 1 tablespoon brandy
- Salt and pepper, to taste

- Fresh chives, for garnish (optional)

Instructions
1. Preheat your air fryer to 375°F (190°C) for 5 minutes.
2. Air Fry your seasoned lobster meat.
3. In a skillet, melt the butter over medium heat. Add the chopped onion and minced garlic. Sauté until they become translucent.
4. Stir in the tomato paste and cook for an additional 2 minutes.
5. Pour in the brandy and simmer until it reduces by half.
6. Add the seafood or fish broth and bring the mixture to a boil. Reduce the heat and let it simmer for 5 minutes.
7. Remove the skillet from the heat and carefully transfer the mixture to a blender. Blend until smooth.
8. Return the blended mixture to the skillet. Stir in the heavy cream and lobster meat. Season with salt and pepper. Simmer for another 5 minutes until heated through.
9. Pour the lobster bisque into two serving bowls.
10. Optionally, garnish with fresh chives before serving.

Air-Fried Cider-Glazed Scallops

Serves 2/Prep time: 10 minutes / Cook Time: 10 minutes | Calories: 250 | Fats: 10g | Carbs: 15g | Fiber: 0g | Protein: 20g

- 200g fresh scallops
- 2 tablespoons olive oil
- 60ml apple cider
- 2 tablespoons brown sugar
- 1 teaspoon Dijon mustard
- Salt and pepper, to taste
- Fresh parsley, for garnish (optional)

Instructions
1. Preheat your air fryer to 375°F (190°C) for 5 minutes.
2. In a bowl, whisk together the apple cider, brown sugar, and Dijon mustard until well combined. Set aside.
3. Season the fresh scallops with salt and pepper.
4. In a skillet, heat the olive oil over medium-high heat. Add the scallops and sear for 1-2 minutes on each side until they develop a golden crust.
5. Pour the cider mixture over the seared scallops.
6. Carefully transfer the scallops and cider mixture to the air fryer basket.
7. Air fry the scallops for 5-6 minutes at 375°F (190°C) until the cider glaze thickens and the scallops are cooked through.
8. Serve the cider-glazed scallops in individual plates.
9. Optionally, garnish with fresh parsley before serving.

Air-Fried Seafood Gumbo

Serves 2 /Prep time: 20 minutes / Cook Time: 25 minutes | Calories: 300 | Fats: 10g | Carbs: 30g | Fiber: 4g | Protein: 20g

- 200g shrimp, peeled and deveined
- 200g crab meat
- 100g okra, sliced
- 1/2 green bell pepper, chopped (50g)
- 50g onion, chopped
- 10g garlic, minced
- 30g all-purpose flour
- 2 tablespoons vegetable oil
- 480ml seafood or chicken broth
- 240g crushed tomatoes
- 1 bay leaf
- 1 teaspoon gumbo file powder
- 1/2 teaspoon paprika
- 1/2 teaspoon dried thyme
- Salt and pepper, to taste
- Cooked rice, for serving
- Fresh parsley, for garnish (optional)

Instructions

1. In a skillet, heat the vegetable oil over medium heat. Add the chopped green bell pepper and onion. Sauté until they become translucent.
2. Stir in the minced garlic, all-purpose flour, paprika, dried thyme, salt, and pepper. Cook for an additional 2 minutes, stirring constantly to create a roux.
3. Gradually pour in the seafood or chicken broth while stirring continuously to create a thick gumbo base.
4. Add the crushed tomatoes, bay leaf, gumbo file powder, and sliced okra. Simmer for 10-15 minutes until the okra is tender.
5. Preheat your air fryer to 375°F (190°C) for 5 minutes.
6. Using an Air Fryer dish, pour this into the dish and place in the preheated air fryer.
7. Put in the crab meat and shrimp. Cook for an additional 5-7 minutes until the shrimp turn pink and the crab meat is heated through.
8. Remove the bay leaf before serving.
9. Serve the seafood gumbo over cooked rice.
10. Optionally, garnish with fresh parsley before serving.

Air-Fried Fisherman's Basket (Assorted Seafood)

Serves 2 /Prep time: 15 minutes / Cook Time: 15 minutes   Calories: 400 | Fats: 10g | Carbs: 40g | Fiber: 2g | Protein: 30g

- For the Assorted Seafood:
- 200g white fish fillets, cut into strips
- 150g calamari rings
- 150g shrimp, peeled and deveined
- 1/2 cup all-purpose flour (60g)
- 2 eggs, beaten (100g)
- 1 cup breadcrumbs (100g)
- Salt and pepper, to taste
- Lemon wedges, for garnish (optional)

Instructions

1. Preheat your air fryer to 375°F (190°C) for 5 minutes.
2. Season the assorted seafood with salt and pepper.
3. Set up a breading station with three shallow bowls: one with all-purpose flour, one with beaten

eggs, and one with breadcrumbs.
4. Dip each piece of seafood into the flour, then into the beaten eggs, and finally into the breadcrumbs, pressing the breadcrumbs onto the seafood to adhere.
5. Place the breaded seafood in the air fryer basket.
6. Air fry the assorted seafood for 10-12 minutes at 375°F (190°C) until they are golden brown and crispy.
7. Serve with lemon wedges if desired.

Air-Fried Pork and Apple Sausage Rolls

Serves 2 /Prep time: 20 minutes / Cook Time: 18 minutes   Calories: 600 | Fat: 42g | Carbs: 35g | Fiber: 2g | Protein: 18g

- 300g pork sausages, casings removed
- 100g apple, peeled and finely chopped
- 50g onion, finely chopped
- 1/2 teaspoon dried sage
- Salt and pepper, to taste
- 200g puff pastry
- 1 egg, beaten
- Cooking spray or oil, for air frying

Instructions
1. Preheat your air fryer to 375°F (190°C) for 5 minutes.
2. In a bowl, combine the pork sausage meat, chopped apple, chopped onion, dried sage, salt, and pepper. Mix well.
3. Roll out the puff pastry and cut it into two equal rectangles.
4. Divide the sausage mixture in half and shape it into two long sausages that fit the length of each puff pastry rectangle.
5. Place each sausage on a puff pastry rectangle and roll the pastry around the sausage, sealing the edges with a bit of beaten egg.
6. Brush the top of each pastry with more beaten egg for a golden finish.
7. Spray the air fryer basket with cooking spray or lightly oil it to prevent sticking.
8. Place the sausage rolls in the air fryer basket.
9. Air fry the sausage rolls for 18-20 minutes at 375°F (190°C) until the pastry is golden brown and the sausages are cooked through.

Air-Fried Beef and Ale Stew

Serves 2 /Prep time: 20 minutes / Cook Time: 30 minutes   Calories: 500 | Fat: 20g | Carbs: 30g | Fiber: 4g | Protein: 35g

- 300g beef stew meat, cubed
- 50g onion, finely chopped
- 10g garlic, minced
- 100g carrot, peeled and sliced
- 150g potato, peeled and diced
- 1 tablespoon all-purpose flour
- 240ml ale or stout beer
- 120ml beef broth
- Salt and pepper, to taste
- Cooking spray or oil, for air frying

Instructions
1. Preheat your air fryer to 375°F (190°C) for 5 minutes.
2. In a skillet, heat a little oil over medium-high heat. Add the beef stew meat and brown it on all sides. Remove the beef from the skillet and set it aside.

3. In the same skillet, add a bit more oil if needed. Add the chopped onion and garlic. Sauté for 2-3 minutes until they become translucent.
4. Stir in the sliced carrot and diced potato. Cook for an additional 5 minutes.
5. Sprinkle the all-purpose flour over the vegetables and stir well to coat.
6. Add the ale or stout beer and beef broth to the skillet. Stir until the mixture thickens.
7. Return the browned beef to the skillet and season with salt and pepper. Simmer for 10-15 minutes until the beef is tender.
8. While the stew is simmering, spray the air fryer basket with cooking spray or lightly oil it to prevent sticking.
9. Place the stew in the air fryer basket.
10. Air fry the stew for 10-12 minutes at 375°F (190°C) until the top is golden brown and the stew is hot and bubbling.

Air-Fried Chicken Balti

Serves 2 /Prep time: 25 minutes / Cook Time: 20 minutes Calories: 400 | Fat: 20g | Carbs: 20g | Fiber: 3g | Protein: 35g

- 300g boneless, skinless chicken thighs, diced
- 100g onion, finely chopped
- 10g garlic, minced
- 1 tablespoon ginger-garlic paste
- 2 tablespoons balti curry paste
- 120g canned chopped tomatoes
- 120ml chicken broth
- 60g plain yogurt
- Salt and pepper, to taste
- Cooking spray or oil, for air frying

Instructions
1. Preheat your air fryer to 375°F (190°C) for 5 minutes.
2. In a skillet, heat a little oil over medium-high heat. Add the chopped onion and sauté for 2-3 minutes until it becomes translucent.
3. Add the minced garlic and ginger-garlic paste to the skillet. Cook for another minute until fragrant.
4. Stir in the balti curry paste and cook for 2-3 minutes, stirring continuously.
5. Add the diced chicken thighs to the skillet and brown them on all sides.
6. Pour in the canned chopped tomatoes, chicken broth, and plain yogurt. Stir well and simmer for 10 minutes until the chicken is cooked through and the sauce thickens. Season with salt and pepper.
7. While the chicken is simmering, spray the air fryer basket with cooking spray or lightly oil it to prevent sticking.
8. Place the Chicken Balti in the air fryer basket.
9. Air fry the Chicken Balti for 10-12 minutes at 375°F (190°C) until it's heated through and the top is slightly crispy.

Air-Fried Mushroom and Stilton Pies

Serves 2 /Prep time: 25 minutes / Cook Time: 18 minutes Calories: 600 | Fat: 45g | Carbs: 35g | Fiber: 2g | Protein: 15g

- For the Filling:
- 200g mushrooms, sliced
- 100g onion, finely chopped
- 10g garlic, minced
- 100g Stilton cheese, crumbled

- 60g heavy cream
- Salt and pepper, to taste
- For the Pastry:
- 200g puff pastry
- 1 egg, beaten
- Cooking spray or oil, for air frying

Instructions

1. Preheat your air fryer to 375°F (190°C) for 5 minutes.
2. In a skillet, heat a little oil over medium heat. Add the chopped onion and sauté for 2-3 minutes until it becomes translucent.
3. Add the minced garlic and sliced mushrooms to the skillet. Cook for 5-7 minutes until the mushrooms are tender and browned.
4. Stir in the crumbled Stilton cheese and heavy cream. Season with salt and pepper. Cook for another 2-3 minutes until the cheese melts and the mixture thickens. Remove from heat.
5. Roll out the puff pastry and cut it into two equal circles.
6. Place each pastry circle in the bottom of two air fryer-safe dishes.
7. Divide the mushroom and Stilton filling between the two dishes, covering the pastry.
8. Brush the top of each pastry with beaten egg for a golden finish.
9. Spray the air fryer basket with cooking spray or lightly oil it to prevent sticking.
10. Place the mushroom and Stilton pies in the air fryer basket.
11. Air fry the pies for 16-18 minutes at 375°F (190°C) until the pastry is golden brown and the filling is hot and bubbly.

Air-Fried Salmon and Dill Fishcakes

Serves 2 /Prep time: 25 minutes / Cook Time: 16 minutes   Calories: 350 | Fat: 10g | Carbs: 40g | Fiber: 3g | Protein: 25g

- 200g salmon fillet, cooked and flaked
- 200g potatoes, boiled and mashed
- 1 small onion, finely chopped (100g)
- 2 tablespoons fresh dill, chopped (10g)
- Zest and juice of 1 lemon
- Salt and pepper, to taste
- 1 egg, beaten (50g)
- 1 cup breadcrumbs (100g)
- Cooking spray or oil, for air frying

Instructions

1. Preheat your air fryer to 375°F (190°C) for 5 minutes.
2. In a bowl, combine the flaked salmon, mashed potatoes, chopped onion, chopped dill, lemon zest, and lemon juice. Season with salt and pepper. Mix well.
3. Divide the mixture into four portions and shape them into fishcake patties.
4. Dip each fishcake into the beaten egg and then coat it in breadcrumbs, pressing the breadcrumbs onto the fishcakes to adhere.
5. Spray the air fryer basket with cooking spray or lightly oil it to prevent sticking.
6. Place the salmon and dill fishcakes in the air fryer basket.
7. Air fry the fishcakes for 14-16 minutes at 375°F (190°C) until they are golden brown and heated through.

INDEX

A
Air-Fried Bacon-Wrapped Asparagus Soldiers 66
Air-Fried Baked Beans on Toast   66
Air-Fried Beef and Ale Stew 73
Air-Fried Chicken Balti   74
Air-Fried Cider-Glazed Scallops   71
Air-Fried Cream Cheese Bagels   67
Air-Fried English Muffins with   66
Air-Fried Fisherman's Basket (Assorted Seafood)   72
Air-Fried Kedgeree   67
Air-Fried Lamb Chops with Rosemary and Mint Sauce   68
Air-Fried Lamb Chump   68
Air-Fried Lobster Bisque   70
Air-Fried Mushroom and Stilton Pies 74
Air-Fried Pork and Apple Sausage Rolls   73
Air-Fried Pork Loin with Apple Compote   69
Air-Fried Salmon and Dill Fishcakes 75
Air-Fried Seafood Gumbo   71
Air-Fried Smoked Salmon and Cream Cheese Pinwheels   70
Apple Muffins 41
Arancini Balls 42
Aromatic Coconut Oatmeal   43

B
Bacon-Wrapped Scallops   59
Baked Beans with Chorizo   45
Baked Bhajis 41
Baked Breaded Mushrooms   50
Baked Chicken Fajitas   19
Baked Chicken Nuggets   18
Banana Muffins   65
Banana Mug Cake   63
Barbecued Vegan "Chicken" 52
BBQ Point end Brisket   26
BBQ Tempeh Salad   51
Bourbon Bread Pudding   39
Breakfast Bars with Seeds   12
Breakfast Burrito Bowl   12
Breakfast Masala Frittata   13
British Chelsea Bun   10
British Pork Sandwich   23
Burnt Butter Cabbage 55
Butternut Squash Mash   58

C
Cajun Chicken Traybake   16
Cajun King Prawn   57
Cajun Lentil and Quinoa   48
Caramelized Plums   62
Cauliflower Fritters   59
Cheddar Cornbread Mini Loaves   39
Cheese Stuffed Mushrooms   56
Chicken and Halloumi Burgers   16
Chicken Bacon Polpettes   19
Chicken Satay Strips 20
Chocolate Brownies   62
Chocolate Cupcakes   65
Chorizo Tomato Pilaf 40
Cinnamon Apple Fritters   64
Classic Carnitas   26
Classic Roast Fish   33
Corned Beef Hash   29
Courgette and Sweetcorn Fritters   48
Cranberry-Glazed Roast Turkey   20
Crispy Bacon Hash Browns   11
Crunchy Popcorn Chicken   60

D
Double Bean Vegetarian Chilli   47

E
Easy Fried Prawns   32
Easy Macaroni Cheese   42
Easy Marinated Swordfish   34
Eggy Bread with a Twist   9
English Mustard Roast Chicken   21

F
Fish and Potato Croquettes   34
Fried Breaded Squid Rings (Calamari)   31

G
Granola with Cranberries   43
Green Bean and Tofu Salad   50
Grilled Stuffed Aubergine Rolls   51

H
Haggis Potato Cakes with Eggs   13
Herb Chicken Mini Fillets   21
Honey Hot Wings   15

I
Italian Mushroom Risotto   49

L
Lamb Shank with Red Wine Gravy   69
Lemon & Pepper Fish 37
Lime Crusted Fish Fillets   35

M
Millet and Bean Croquettes   44
Mushroom and Bacon Risotto   45

N
Nacho Cheeseburgers 27
Nutty Crusted Fish   37

O
Oat Biscuits   44
Oat Pots with Berries and Almonds   10
Old-Fashioned Meatballs   24
Orange-Glazed Duck Breast   17

P
Paprika Okra Chips   55
Paprika Parmesan Sweet Potatoes   49
Paprika Pork Medallions   28
Parmesan Pork Chops 23
Peanut Butter Cookies   64
Plum Flapjack Crumble   63
Potato Rösti   56
Prawn Katsu   36
Prawn Wontons   40
Prune & Gorgonzola Polenta Stacks   11
Pumpkin English Muffins   9

Q
Quinoa and Chickpea Patties 52

R
Red Beet Salad   57
Roasted Tuna with Olives   35
Roast Fillet of Sea Bass   31
Roast Pork Belly   25
Roast Turkey Breast   17
Rump Steak with Gorgonzola 28

S
Salmon and Asparagus Traybake   36
Savoury Mince Muffins   29
Sizzling Spare Ribs   25
Spiced Devilled Eggs 8
Spicy Mini Meatloaves   27
Spicy Sweet Potato Chips   58
Sticky Garlic Trout   33

T
Tandoori-ish Chicken Thighs 15
Turkey Chorizo Ragù 18
Turkey Crown with Cranberry Glaze 68
Two Grain Baked Porridge   8

V
Vegan Bean "Meatballs"   47
Vegan Burritos   53

W
Warm Spicy Salmon Salad   32
Warm Steak Salad   24

MEASUREMENT CONVERSION CHART

VOLUME EQUIVALENTS(DRY)

US STANDARD	METRIC (APPROXIMATE)
1/8 teaspoon	0.5 mL
1/4 teaspoon	1 mL
1/2 teaspoon	2 mL
3/4 teaspoon	4 mL
1 teaspoon	5 mL
1 tablespoon	15 mL
1/4 cup	59 mL
1/2 cup	118 mL
3/4 cup	177 mL
1 cup	235 mL
2 cups	475 mL
3 cups	700 mL
4 cups	1 L

WEIGHT EQUIVALENTS

US STANDARD	METRIC (APPROXIMATE)
1 ounce	28 g
2 ounces	57 g
5 ounces	142 g
10 ounces	284 g
15 ounces	425 g
16 ounces (1 pound)	455 g
1.5 pounds	680 g
2 pounds	907 g

VOLUME EQUIVALENTS(LIQUID)

US STANDARD	US STANDARD (OUNCES)	METRIC (APPROXIMATE)
2 tablespoons	1 fl.oz.	30 mL
1/4 cup	2 fl.oz.	60 mL
1/2 cup	4 fl.oz.	120 mL
1 cup	8 fl.oz.	240 mL
1 1/2 cup	12 fl.oz.	355 mL
2 cups or 1 pint	16 fl.oz.	475 mL
4 cups or 1 quart	32 fl.oz.	1 L
1 gallon	128 fl.oz.	4 L

TEMPERATURES EQUIVALENTS

FAHRENHEIT(F)	CELSIUS(C) (APPROXIMATE)
225 °F	107 °C
250 °F	120 °C
275 °F	135 °C
300 °F	150 °C
325 °F	160 °C
350 °F	180 °C
375 °F	190 °C
400 °F	205 °C
425 °F	220 °C
450 °F	235 °C
475 °F	245 °C
500 °F	260 °C

The Dirty Dozen and Clean Fifteen

The Environmental Working Group (EWG) is a nonprofit, nonpartisan organization dedicated to protecting human health and the environment Its mission is to empower people to live healthier lives in a healthier environment. This organization publishes an annual list of the twelve kinds of produce, in sequence, that have the highest amount of pesticide residue-the Dirty Dozen-as well as a list of the fifteen kinds ofproduce that have the least amount of pesticide residue-the Clean Fifteen.

THE DIRTY DOZEN

- The 2016 Dirty Dozen includes the following produce. These are considered among the year's most important produce to buy organic:

Strawberries	Spinach
Apples	Tomatoes
Nectarines	Bell peppers
Peaches	Cherry tomatoes
Celery	Cucumbers
Grapes	Kale/collard greens
Cherries	Hot peppers

- The Dirty Dozen list contains two additional itemskale/collard greens and hot peppers-because they tend to contain trace levels of highly hazardous pesticides.

THE CLEAN FIFTEEN

- The least critical to buy organically are the Clean Fifteen list. The following are on the 2016 list:

Avocados	Papayas
Corn	Kiw
Pineapples	Eggplant
Cabbage	Honeydew
Sweet peas	Grapefruit
Onions	Cantaloupe
Asparagus	Cauliflower
Mangos	

- Some of the sweet corn sold in the United States are made from genetically engineered (GE) seedstock. Buy organic varieties of these crops to avoid GE produce.

Printed in Great Britain
by Amazon